# From There to

## Sixteen True Tales of Immigration to Britain: The Second decibel Penguin Prize Anthology

PENGUIN BOOKS

PENGUIN BOOKS

Published by the Penguin Group
Penguin Books Ltd, 80 Strand, London WC2R ORL, England
Penguin Group (USA) Inc., 375 Hudson Street, New York, New York 10014, USA
Penguin Group (Canada), 90 Eglinton Avenue East, Suite 700, Toronto, Ontario, Canada M4P 2Y3
(a division of Pearson Penguin Canada Inc.)
Penguin Ireland, 25 St Stephen's Green, Dublin 2, Ireland
(a division of Penguin Books Ltd)
Penguin Group (Australia), 250 Camberwell Road, Camberwell, Victoria 3124, Australia
(a division of Pearson Australia Group Pty Ltd)
Penguin Books India Pvt Ltd, 11 Community Centre, Panchsheel Park, New Delhi – 110 017, India
Penguin Group (NZ), 67 Apollo Drive, Rosedale, North Shore 0632, New Zealand
(a division of Pearson New Zealand Ltd)
Penguin Books (South Africa) (Pty) Ltd, 24 Sturdee Avenue, Rosebank, Johannesburg 2196, South Africa

Penguin Books Ltd, Registered Offices: 80 Strand, London WC2R ORL, England

www.penguin.com

First published in Penguin Books 2007
1

Selection copyright © Penguin Books, 2007
Copyright for each piece lies with individual authors © 2007
All rights reserved

The moral right of the authors has been asserted

With acknowledgements to decibel and Arts Council England

Set in 12.75/15.5 pt Monotype Dante
Typeset by Rowland Phototypesetting Ltd, Bury St Edmunds, Suffolk
Printed in England by Clays Ltd, St Ives plc

ISBN: 978-0-141-03411-9

# Contents

# Immigrant

*Menaka Raman*

I am migrant.
I'm migrant.
Im-migrant.
Immigrant.

I like to think that this is how the word immigrant was created. It seems kinder. It takes the harshness and edge off a word that can so easily sound abusive. It makes me feel like a bird that has temporarily flown the nest, meaning to return home one day. Albeit a rather foolish bird that has confused the concept of migration, leaving a warm land for one that is decidedly not. Perhaps that's why, at first, I was floundering in the plumage department, my feathers ill-equipped for the country I found myself in.

When I told my mother about my impending move to London, one of the first things she said was, 'Oh, how wonderful! I'll bring down all the coats and sweaters.'

My family had lived in London many years ago, and like most Indians, who are loath to part with things, we still owned box upon box of possessions we had no use for in Madras (though with the weather behaving as it has lately, perhaps the southern states of India will one day see snow). A common refrain heard in our home was: 'Let it be. You never know when we will need it.' As you can imagine, we rarely managed to clear the clutter.

Though I'm sure a maternal desire to prevent her youngest child from freezing in winter was a motivating factor, I had a niggling suspicion that my mother was mainly eyeing the soon-to-be-empty space for the reserves in her ever-growing army of Tupperware boxes.

'Think of all the money you'll save,' Mother cooed as she shook out ancient sweaters, jackets and scarves that had all seen better decades. Grateful that I wouldn't need to rub goose fat over my body to stay warm, I took all that was offered, telling myself that fashion was cyclical, retro was in. I might even set a new trend in the red and black chequered puffer jacket that occasionally coughed up swan feathers through a small, invisible tear in the sleeve.

Bearing these family heirlooms, a pressure cooker, a saucepan, a ladle, a silver Ganesha and a few clothes, my husband and I arrived at Heathrow Airport on a sunny Sunday afternoon in October (the weather a final gift bequeathed by the month before it passed on). I was relieved – it meant I didn't have to take my jacket out of the suitcase. Where it would stay till my lips turned blue, I decided when we arrived at our temporary accommodation, a tiny matchbox of a hotel room on Old Brompton Road. God was fond of cruel jokes, I realized, as I found myself in one of London's most fashionable quarters looking like an Indian lumberjack. Everywhere we went, my coat and I stuck out like a communist flag, billowing against the virginal white façades of the gated communities in the Royal Borough of Kensington and Chelsea. From the moment I stepped out of our room, I was surrounded by women draped in cashmere, carrying bags that cost more than my life savings, reminding me of how little I belonged.

I tried my best to blend in. A difficult task since nothing I owned matched my jacket. My wardrobe consisted of clothes more suited to sunnier climes. Crinkled cotton skirts in shocking pinks and coppersulphate blues, hems weighed down by tiny, jingling bells. Salwar kameezes in *kalamkari* and *ikkat* prints. Wearing these teamed with my jacket, I resembled a bag lady on acid. In an effort to fit in, I purchased a tartan-ish cape. In pink and purple. Made of mohair. If anyone has ever looked at something on a mannequin in a depressed and delusional frame of mind and thought it was just the thing to cheer them up, perhaps they will understand what prompted me to purchase such a creation. Convinced that I'd discovered the look of the season, I took home what now resembles a multi-coloured dust bunny. Cape in hand, I was ready to let the rest of the world see just how fashionable I could be. I fished out a pair of black trousers, a green and blue striped shirt and an ancient red sweater, and fastened the mohair cape around my neck. If I ever become a superhero (though I doubt I will be allowed to fight crimes against fashion), I will probably choose to look as I did that day – a startling cross between William Wallace and Phoolan Devi. Blissfully unaware of the anxious glances from passers-by and the mothers who shielded their children from the abominable pink snowlady, I walked – I must admit – rather jauntily to the station and boarded a train. Crammed in with the usual commuter mix, I wedged myself between two dark-suited City types. Their noses, which had been buried in the *FT* till I arrived, soon began to twitch and I found myself (or rather my cape) the cause of a sneezing storm. I was fated to look like a Maoist lumberjack for ever.

We soon moved into our own home. Eager to live in a 'proper' English house (with a downstairs and an upstairs) and yet desiring easy access to fresh coriander leaves and cumin-flavoured *papads*, we moved to Harrow in north-west London. The semi-detached we rented and the strong Asian community in the area ticked our two boxes. I felt more at home in Harrow. Less intimidated. Why, next to the wrinkled Gujarati grandmothers in their soft cotton saris, feet encased in Birkenstocks and socks, bent over under the weight of the enormous coats that swamped their frail bodies, I even looked stylish.

As the excitement of living in a new city slowly wore off, homesickness set in along with the dark winter evenings. I began to miss home, my parents, my life. I missed sunshine and palm trees and soft breezes that carried aloft the fragrance of tamarind. I missed bare shoulders and the feel of soft *mul-mul* against my skin. I didn't feel like me any more – it was as though all those layers of clothes were suffo-cating my true self. I became sullen and morose, envious of the men and women frolicking around palm trees in the old 1980s movies the Indian cable channels showed. I stopped going out. Sitting next to the window by the radiator and looking at the empty street outside the house became my favourite pas-time. Until our boiler bust. As I sat shivering inside the house, I was forced to turn to the only comrade I had left – my mother's coat. In the week it took to repair our boiler, I grew to love that coat, feather-coughing tear and all.

The coat and other hand-me-downs that had seen my mother through similar winters carried me through those initial lonely months. The oversized candy-striped cardigan with shiny plastic buttons down the front, the lime-green V-neck jumper and my father's beige sweater-vest in a way stood in for my absent family. Wrapped in those garments, I felt closer to home.

It's been over two years since we came to London and I'm glad to say I've settled down well. I work. I've made friends. I have some very nice winter coats. But I find that in those occasional moments of home-sickness slipping into my mother's jacket or my father's sweater is as comforting as being enveloped in their warm embraces. I may not be migrating back to warmer climes for some time, but till then I have found a way of keeping my old home as close to me as possible.

Some time ago, as my husband and I sorted through our clothes looking for things to give to charity, he pulled out the lumberjack coat and said, 'What do you want this for? Get rid of it.'

'Let it be,' I replied. 'You never know when we will need it.'

# Son of a *Hoca*

*Cosh Omar*

*Hoca* is pronounced 'Hoja'.

Being the son of an imam wasn't easy. It wasn't common either. I was born into the Turkish-Cypriot community in north London. To most of the Islamic world, the Turkish-Cypriots aren't even Muslims. They have drifted so far from the faith that most of them don't even know their daily prayers. But not my family, oh no. When I was a child, my parents seemed to me to be the only practising Turkish-Cypriot Muslims in the world. None of my uncles or aunties, either in London or in Cyprus, were practising. I had no cousins that were practising. I had family that were Turkish 'nationalists' and some that were 'socialists', but absolutely none that were practising Muslims. In fact, I wasn't familiar with the word 'practising' till I was all grown-up and practising myself. My parents were just different and, well, Muslim. I knew the rest of the community respected my parents, though. I say 'respected'; what I mean is that they needed them.

Whenever there was a death in a family, it was my parents who were called in to do the prayers, which took place in the form of a Mevlid. This is an old Sufi practice from the twelfth century that first celebrated the Prophet Muhammad's birthday but was then used at circumcisions, deaths and any occasion one wanted, really. But by the time I was born, the Turkish-Cypriots of London mostly had a Mevlid for a death or for the birth of a daughter. (The celebrations for a son were usually saved for a circumcision party that took place later on in his life, and this was always an alcohol-soaked affair and not very 'practising' at all.) The Mevlid always took place in some Turkish-Cypriot home. My mum and dad would sit at one end of a room that was full mostly of women who, for this time only, I would see wearing headscarves – but not full *hijabs*, as we are now accustomed to seeing young Muslim women wearing; oh no, these were just see-through rayon numbers that were fashionably draped over their 1970s bouffant hairdos. As most of the lower floor of the house was rammed with these women covered in rayon, the men would occupy a room upstairs or, if it was a pleasant evening, the garden, and as the ancient Islamic Sufi rite inspired by the great Rumi took place inside, they would slowly get drunk on raki outside. I myself always sat inside. This wasn't just to dodge the alcohol-induced jibes made at my parents' expense for being practising Muslims; I genuinely enjoyed the Mevlid. It was so beautifully dramatic.

My parents would always have a small side table

respectfully placed in front of them, with two glasses of water to soothe their throats throughout the Mevlid. On the table they would place the Holy Koran and various sheets of paper. On these sheets of paper were a number of poems either that they had written themselves or that were passed down through the history of Sufism, and also notes on the family, such as the name of the deceased and both parents' names. Then, when the full house had quietened down and all was ready, my parents would begin. Both, with their great voices, would sing the celebrated text of Suleyman Celebi from the fourteenth to the fifteenth centuries, in which Celebi explains the superiority of Prophet Muhammad over all other prophets, in six sections that make the Mevlid. The whole thing consists of approximately eight hundred couplets in the metre in the *mesnevi* style, a rhymed couplet. The first section is 'Munacat', the rogation to Allah. The second is 'Veladet' and tells of the birth of Prophet Muhammad. The third is 'Risalet', the coming of the first revelation. This is followed by 'Mi'rac', which celebrates the miracle of the Prophet's ascent to heaven. The second from last is 'Rihlet', the death of Prophet Muhammad, and lastly, 'Dua', the forgiving of sin and Prophet Muhammad's wish for salvation. At various points, a couple of young girls would be asked to go round the congregation and pour rose water into everyone's hands from elaborate sprinklers. The tradition was to rub the rose water into your hands and pass them over your face. Although I detested the thought of rubbing rose water into my face, I do remember enjoying the sweet smell of roses that filled the house along with the sound of my parents' voices. To bring the Mevlid to an end, my parents would check their notes for the deceased's name, and both parents' names, and then ask the congregation to recite the first *surah* of the Holy Koran, 'Al Fatiha', for his or her soul. It was this part that had a profound effect on my attitude towards death, even now. In Arabic, *'al fatiha'* means 'the beginning' or 'the opening', and after crying their way through the recitation, the congregation would be informed by my parents that death has no rule of order in its choice. That although we would like it that way and are accustomed to believe that parents should die before their offspring, that a certain age is too young to die, that it is unfair for a child to be left without the love of the departed mother or father, death comes to those whose time it is to pass on. Sitting there by my parents, hearing their words, my eyes would always be fixed on the numerous photographs that had been put up in loving memory of the deceased. Those photographs changed nearly every day of my childhood. One evening, they would be of an elderly grandmother or grandfather – however elderly, he or she would still have a mourning child in the room.

Another evening, they would be of a child with an innocent smile or a teenager with all the hope of life in his or her eyes. It was those photographs that instilled in me the knowledge that, yes, any life has a beginning, a middle and an end, but just how long that life will be is not for us to know. With each Mevlid, I knew we were all stepping forwards in a queue towards our own end, but just where we were in that queue nobody knew, no matter what their faith.

Once the Mevlid was over, my parents would turn to their own poems, which, like Suleyman Celebi's Mevlid and most Sufi poetry, were written to be sung at gatherings (such poems are called *ilahi* and are a bit like hymns). By far my favourite of these was one that my mother wrote at the age of thirteen, after the death of her own mother, my grandmother, Ayse, or, as I know her, Ayse nene. In the poem, my mother talks of how she saw Ayse nene's dead body in her bed and yet was not afraid to kiss her pale face and wrap her arms around her. She wonders who will now tuck her into bed and read fairy tales to her. Who will she now tell her problems to and seek such loving empathy from? And she questions why Ayse nene died and left her child behind, how such a beautiful life could come to such an abrupt end. She closes the poem with a wish that Ayse nene's soul is at peace and that this peace is not disturbed by the smell of the soil that her body now lies in. My mother would normally sing this poem at a Mevlid when the deceased was a mother and the house was full of her children and sometimes grandchildren. At many Mevlids, my mother would be requested to sing this *ilahi*. The effect was breathtaking. To this day I can remember the box of man-size Kleenex that would be passed round and how it would empty in seconds. But the best part was not seeing the rayon-covered women cry. By the late 1970s, all Turkish-Cypriots, like most of the British nation, had pulled down any separating walls to create what they thought were fashionable through-lounges, and from my seat next to my mother and father at one end of the house, I could see all the way to the other side. Standing there, with their bloodshot faces pressed against the ugly, newly installed, double-glazed patio doors, their raki-reeking breath leaving condensation on the glass, were the men. I could see the tears pouring down their cheeks. The jibes against my parents were no longer to be heard. There was nothing but emotional clarity. Or was it hysteria? Who cares? My parents had them all in the palms of their rose-water-drenched hands. This full house, usually more than two hundred people – that's bigger than some of the houses I've played to as an actor – was completely, emotionally at one with my parents. I loved it.

They always gave a great performance and because

of that, and because of who they were, they were respected throughout the Turkish-Cypriot community. Our house was always full of people coming to ask my parents' advice on a number of personal subjects. Sometimes it was the elderly complaining about the young and sometimes it was the rebellious young who'd had enough of the controlling old. And through the whole thing there was always little old me, sitting there mostly silent, listening to all the gory details. It was fantastic. But it was at the Mevlids, every night, that my parents really came into their own. And it was at the Mevlids, in those moments of emotional clarity, those few moments when the Mevlid had finished and the young girls had put down their rose water sprinklers and were handing out Turkish delight on elaborate trays, that I too felt at one with the rest of the community. For those few moments, I had something in common with them and they understood my world, a world where Islam played some part. And for those few moments, they respected Islam and therefore respected me. I was the son of the imam. But the Turkish-Cypriots don't use the word imam much. They use the word '*hoca*', which means teacher. I was the son of the *hoca*.

# Bluebird

*Vesna Maric*

The day we left was a hot September morning, after a night of torn sleep. A crowd of seventy or eighty people stood on the seafront, besieged by suitcases, getting ready to board the two coaches. We were mainly women and children. The men were waiting around to say goodbye to their wives; a couple had managed to evade the draft somehow and were coming along. I stood with my distraught mother, watching the playful ripple of the Adriatic. Outside the buses, bustling around and already a little red from the autumn sun, were the British. They had come to take us away from our dusty old towns, where things lately had not been so good.

The journey had been cooked up by a children's organization, and Milan, who was in liaison with Derek, a bookshop-owner from the north of England, was in charge of us – a 'manager', as he liked to be known. None of us knew where exactly it was we were going. All that Milan had told us was to dress down, to look as bad as possible, because the group before, he said, had been too dressed up. The British had complained that they didn't really look like refugees. Milan had described it to my mother the week before, over the telephone: 'They looked as if they were dressed up for a wedding.' I imagined my vain compatriots in their Italian fashion suits, rescued from their homes with lipstick and eyeshadow intact, like armour.

The British had, understandably, expected something a little more like 'proper' refugees: people obviously suffering, hardship visible on their faces, clothes torn and wrinkled, children's eyes stuck with crusty tears. Milan was weaving himself through the crowd, closely inspecting everyone's outfits by pinching a shirt, a skirt or a trouser leg between two fingers, rubbing it to feel its quality, a look of disgust on his face. But the unspoken motto of these Bosnian mothers was: 'If we are going to be refugees, let's not advertise our misery, let us at least look good,' and I could understand how they felt. It's not easy suddenly becoming a refugee.

I was struggling with this idea. I had spent my entire life being just me, belonging to a family, judged mainly by my freckly face or dodgy relatives. But I had never been pitied before, until the word 'refugee' was uttered, and like the rest of the women I was horrified. I was only sixteen and without preconceptions. But here I was, about to become a foreigner. My entire life was going to change.

The time came to board the coach, a time still too

sore to remember. My mother's face was flooded behind my own rivers of tears, and between us a smeared windowpane denoted the first of many obstacles. The bus smelled perhaps of England, and I thought I would never see my mother again or smell the Adriatic Sea that framed her curled hair. The bus engine grumbled, not wanting to move from the comfort of the sun.

There were children on the bus, making posters that read: 'We are the Bosnian refugees!', 'Bosnia and Herzegovina ♥ England!' and 'We love Penrith!' I asked the children if they knew where Penrith was. They said, 'No,' and continued to draw a picture of a bus that was supposed to resemble the one we were on, holding on to the white paper with little fingers stained with red, green and blue marker pens. I faced the asphalt unwinding before us, trying to avoid looking at anything that might make me cry, like trees, mountains or the sea.

We spent nights sleeping at petrol stations, the coaches parked by the flickering neon signs. I woke up and saw the neons glaring at me, as if to say, 'Wake up, wake up!', like a bully. For the first few seconds, I never knew who I was or where I was. I looked around at the sleeping faces, heads suspended like wilting flowers, necks weakened by sleep. A jumble of bodies lay entangled on the back seat. Some looked like they were dreaming about something nasty, their faces grimacing in disapproval. I looked out of the steamed-up window at the occasional cars shooting past, lights leaving a fiery trail behind them.

The morning was filled with the smell of petrol, traffic fumes and dusty seats. A faint smell of coffee struggled on to the bus. Out of the window, the small kitchen in the second bus was visible, but I could only see an arm stirring a beige liquid vigorously and tapping a teaspoon on the edge of a cup, as if about to conduct an orchestra. Our first English coffee, instant, weak and served in massive cups (I later learnt they were called 'mugs', like ugly faces and robbing), was received with ungrateful spits and shouts of: 'This is not coffee! This is piss!' The British laughed in embarrassment. A few people pretended they liked the coffee, not to offend our hosts, saying: 'It tastes like tea!' and grappling for appropriate cultural references. We were used to Turkish coffee, small and strong; coffee that sticks to the floor if you spill it, and tastes like petrol, and whose aroma clings to your palate for hours afterwards.

Italy and Switzerland went past as if they were mere neighbourhoods. I remember Italy only by a small black Fiat huffing up the motorway. In Switzerland, I bought a black lighter with golden hieroglyphics and *'vien avec moi'* written on it. I had no idea what that meant, but it was a souvenir, helping me pretend the journey was just a tourist trip. In France, on the third morning of our journey, tired and cold, I got out of the bus for a cigarette. As I stepped on to the gravel, the luminous white fog of the lowered sky enveloped me. I walked towards a small path, wide enough for one car, just to stretch my legs. There was an old arrow road sign. The paint on it was peeling, and hanging letters read 'PARIS'. I smoked and wondered how far it was down this road and if I started to walk now when I would make it. Everything around me was asleep and white with fog, thick like cotton wool.

The large ferry bobbed on the waves of the Channel, the peeling white paint of the rails sticking to our sweaty, clutching palms as we stared at the foam below. Johnny, the driver, parked the bus alongside all the other vehicles stacked up in the ferry's belly and came upstairs, stretching and shaking off a mild shiver. 'Welcome to England!' he said. 'It's bloody freezing!' He smoothed his frayed moustache over a smile. We stood next to each other like pigeons trying to keep warm, ruffled by the gusts of the wind. All I could think of was the Vera Lynn song. And though I couldn't see bluebirds anywhere, the white cliffs of Dover were becoming visible on the other side, brooding above the grey water, greeting us as if we were Dunkirk evacuees. I watched the outline of the white rocks blend with the sky.

On the fourth day of our journey, we flooded into the Dover immigration office, a cold waiting room with tiled walls and bleak lighting. There was nothing but plastic orange chairs and a poster reminding us what not to do. A man emerged from an office with a face like a scrunched-up fist and thick glasses. He squinted at his clipboard and gave us forms to fill in. Our English hosts helped us through them and those of us who had some English translated for those who had none.

Several hours later, we rolled up towards London. Everything felt different now that we were in Britain. A hollow sense of anticlimax blew through our collective hearts. What now? We approached the big city and went through drab suburbs. Concrete blocks, small identical terraced houses stretching left and right for miles. The bus stopped in front of a grand white house with pillars and steps and 'The Red Cross' neatly engraved on a plaque. The women looked depressed. The reality of our journey suddenly hit home: the Red Cross was all about 'aid', 'disaster', 'war' and 'tragedy'. And we were a product of all those things. This was not a prolonged excursion.

The elegant building, though synonymous with all things sad, was far removed from our Balkan brutality. When I tried to imagine anything to do with the war here, I could only conjure up images from black and white Second World War films: nurses in dresses and square white headgear, soldiers with bandages watching the ceiling. That's what I thought might greet us when we entered the pristine building: we would be ushered into a black and white room with unfolding camp beds and no one would sleep through the grey night.

Instead we found small flower-patterned blankets on the floor, with more knitted blankets on top, the combination of which formed our beds. Everyone looked around, slightly lost, the middle-class émigrés' dignity melting away like ice cream down a cone – no matter how hard they licked, it would all disappear, but at least it tasted good while they had it. Some women sat down on the floor, children asleep in their arms. Some wandered around the place, trying to look like they knew what we were supposed to be doing. One woman found a cardboard box full of soap and picked up a piece that was shaped like an orange. An Englishwoman saw her and jumped up, grabbing the soap from her hand: 'No! Not to eat!' Everyone was aghast: 'How dare she, the bitch! Doesn't she know we had VCRs and cars and soap bars?' Our English hosts were embarrassed by their colleague's odd behaviour, but we understood the situation: they thought we were savages.

Some of the Bosnian women were desperate to convince them otherwise. They spent hours explaining that we used to have everything – beds, sheets, extra linen in the cupboards, embroidered and starched, crystal glasses, memories, china, passports, vacuum cleaners, pets, tastes, holidays, smells, sounds – and most of all that we loved, loved each other, that we hadn't spent the last fifty years secretly hating each other's guts, waiting for the first opportunity to rip each other open in the most savage ways. They wanted to explain that the war was a mistake, a ploy of evil politicians; it wasn't us, the people sitting before them, who had anything to do with its cause.

In the meantime, I had found a small patch on the floor, among the blankets' woolly flowers on the grey office carpet, and decided to go to sleep. There was nothing better to do. I was permanently burdened with a ball in my stomach, a burning feeling that grated on my soul and pressed my throat. As I was getting ready for bed, I saw a woman with grey hair and big glasses stepping carefully through the blankets as if the floor were laden with mines. 'There is an extra bed here,' I told her. 'Oh, thank you,' she smiled, and settled among the flowers. Months later, I lived with this woman and her family in a countryside vicarage, feeling my socialist atheism pulsate while they prayed before each meal. They often prayed for me and my family, for which I was secretly grateful.

Kendal approached us on the final day of our journey, while we slept another uncomfortable, comatose sleep. The white light of the sun, wrapped in a cling-film of thin clouds, woke me and I blinked, trying to adjust to the brightness. Then I saw small cottages, greenery, an emerald countryside, and felt my heart leap. It was beautiful.

The women rolled out of the bus, sleepy and grumpy-faced. The English were chatting away to the Kendal hosts, in front of a small church. Me and a couple of girls who spoke some English were called aside. We were introduced to Brian: a new man. He had a white beard that joined his tufty sideburns and made him look as if he was wearing one of those Santa Claus beard pieces. He spoke slowly and loudly, fixing on us intently as he pronounced: 'WE HAVE SOME CLOTHES INSIDE CHURCH, ALL SORTED FOR EVERYBODY TO LOOK AT AND TAKE WHAT THEY NEED. OR T-SHIRT OR TROUSERS. YES?' (Intense gaze.) 'CAN YOU PLEASE TELL WOMEN GO IN AND LOOK WHEN NO SMOKE? YES?' (Nervous smile.) We went from group to smoking group, informing them.

Cigarettes were crushed under heels that raised dust on the gravel as the women moved towards the church.

The church was small and dark with coloured light peeking through the high stained-glass windows without illuminating the room. The clothes were laid out neatly in a semicircle with a large pile of random items on a long stall in the middle. There were T-shirts of all sizes and lengths, mostly worn out and washed out; trouser legs stuck out their patterns as if fighting for attention; jumpers shone their sequins, revealed their unbuttoned cleavages, beckoned to be chosen. Everything smelled of mothballs and plastic. On a separate wall, in a solitary setting, hung fur coats. Brown, white, ochre, glistening black furs. I knew there would be trouble once they were spotted. Too many Slavic women and too few furs.

Within minutes, the church became a bees' nest, the whirring noise of nimble fingers working through the second-hand items. Some scuffling resounded among the cottons and the nylons; coat hangers made a prudish noise when moved along the metal rail. Temporary chaos filled the House of God when my fur prediction came true. Who was going to get them? Who saw them first? How does one divide charity to become the rightful property of a rightful owner?

'I saw it first,' said one.

'So what? I saw it second.'

'I have a small child. I need a fur coat,' said a woman clutching a sleeping child.

'My surname starts with A and that means I am the first on the alphabetical list.'

'What alphabetical list?'

'They have one, the English. Go ask them if you don't believe me.'

The woman went to enquire about the alphabetical list for getting fur coats. The English had no idea what she was talking about. In the meantime, the 'A' woman stuffed the fur coat into a plastic bag and gave it to her daughter to take on the bus, inconspicuously. She waited in faux fury for the other woman to come back. The English were brought in to rule on who would get a fur coat. After hearing all the emotional appeals for the individual rights to fur, they thought about it for a while, the white-bearded man at their judicial helm looking up at the ceiling as if seeking guidance from God. Finally, he announced: 'Because we cannot decide who gets the fur coats, no one will get one. We shall take them all back into the charity shops, where they will be sold.' The women tried to contest this, but that was the final word. The 'A' woman protested too, to cover up the fact that she'd sneaked off with the fur in the bag.

That day, people were taken one by one or in small groups to have a look at the houses in which they were going to stay. I went to see my future home with my future housemates, Mirjana and her three-year-old son, Sasha. I had been afraid of being put with one of the families and being bossed around by someone else's mother, but Mirjana was twenty-eight and just perfect. We were taken to a house at the end of a long street to meet a woman called Marilyn Wilson. There was a barn in her back garden that had been done up for Marilyn's daughter, Annette, and Annette was giving up the barn for us.

We were introduced to Marilyn's six cats, one of them called Fred, an epileptic who had fits when Marilyn vacuumed her floor. Marilyn seemed to have a thing for adopting the less fortunate. On the first floor of her house lived Philip, a lovely man with Down's syndrome who, according to Marilyn, cried when he saw news reports from Bosnia and was happy to hear we were coming to stay in the house. And then there was Margaret, who had the mental age of a five-year-old. Both she and Philip were extremely cheerful, and as we arrived, there was some commotion because Philip had flushed Margaret's dentures down the toilet. They both thought it was hilarious, but Marilyn was a bit cross.

I started going to school, on the opposite side of town from where I lived with Mirjana, Sasha, Marilyn, Annette, Philip and Margaret, and the six cats. Every morning, I was picked up by a boy from school and his father. The boy didn't talk to me much, he just looked a little pissed off that they had to collect me. I would roll into the car still half asleep and try to mutate into an English-speaker during the ten-minute ride.

The initial months in England were strange. I missed sunlight and was soaked with rain and beaten by northern winds. I took photography classes and photographed fields, trying to capture the rain in the photo frames. I hid in the darkroom, developing prints for hours on end. I socialized sometimes, but mostly I wandered alone. A friend went back to Bosnia after two weeks, and I waved goodbye at the train station with Jude.

Jude worked at the checkout in Safeway, Penrith's biggest supermarket. I went there to see my first big supermarket and was blown away by the choice of margarine. I tried to pick out a hair colour – I wanted a red, but there were so many reds, all offering great things, I couldn't buy any for fear of making the wrong choice. So I picked up a pint of milk and headed for the checkout, and as I queued I saw Jude, in a white uniform, dropping the groceries all over the place, the customers looking irritated. He was smiling at his own clumsiness and I felt an affinity with him immediately. So I went to Safeway a lot and always queued at his till, my heart jumping as he dropped and bruised my fruit and vegetables, smashed my tomatoes. Then one day he asked me if I would meet him for a drink after work.

Out of his supermarket uniform, Jude wore an oversized coat, a pair of old tatty boots and a ruffled shirt, and smoked cigarettes that he rolled himself and that came out in various shapes: pear, banana, cucumber. They never stayed lit, always crumbling and burning holes in his jumper. He fell over everything and I fell in love deeply.

On our evening walks, he asked me about me and we talked. I felt normal, for the first time in a long time. He didn't ask me about dead people, about devastation, didn't display any of the morbid curiosity that so many people did; he asked me about me as if I were a normal girl from Penrith, not one of the Bosnian refugees that everyone talked about. We talked music, The Cure, Neil Young, Tim Buckley, whatever it was we liked. We sang some songs in the dark wet night, the pallid street lights occasionally showing glints of teeth in a smile and the happy eyes of being in love. Jude and I spent a few happy months together, listening to music and reading books. Sometimes we argued, and then I wouldn't pick him up after work outside Safeway. And in December, I went to spend Christmas with him and his family in the countryside.

His house was a cottage sitting alone in a white

snowy field with a frozen lake nearby. The basement was stacked with his father's paintings, one of them displaying the face of Margaret Thatcher in a broken mirror. His father was a kind, bearded man, just how you would expect a countryside artist to look, and his mother had hair down to her waist and spoke in a soft voice. That Christmas has stuck with me for ever – I forgot who I was, why I was there; I forgot that there was a war, that people were dying, that I had no family around me, that I knew nobody. After lunch, we all rested in our bedrooms, I with Jude on his bunk bed on one side of the sitting room – not really a room, more like a train compartment, with a poster of Marilyn Monroe pouting a gentle kiss at us. Jude's father invited us for a walk in the late afternoon, just as the sky was changing from an electric blue to indigo. We went to the lake, which had apparently not frozen over for years until that day. Our hot cheeks burnt in the cold air.

# Culture Shock

*Kirti Joshi*

'Culture Shock' is told from Kirti Joshi's father's point of view.

It was a normal day at the cinema. I remember the sweltering heat and the distinctive smell of fried bananas and plantains. I was listening to the radio as I worked when I heard the announcement that Idi Amin wanted to expel all Asians from Uganda. He was quoted as saying: 'The Asian community are milking the Ugandan cow without feeding it.' This referred to those Asians who sent money to their relatives in different countries. At first, he wanted all the non-citizen Asians to leave, meaning the ones who still had their British passports (this was later expanded to all Ugandan Asians). This shocking statement devastated me. My immediate concerns were for my family, my wife and two daughters, the youngest of whom was only five months old.

Many Asians kept hold of their British passports because Uganda had been under British rule from 1894 to 1962. My parents came from the Gujarat state in India. My father came to Uganda to work, as did many people from India. Uganda became independent on 9 October 1962, and Milton Obote became the first head of state.

It was 5 August 1972, a date that is etched in my memory. We were told we had ninety days to leave. Three things were necessary to leave the country. The first was to have valid travel documents. Secondly, you needed a country of temporary or permanent asylum, and last but not least, you needed money. I knew I had to leave as soon as possible. I had the first two requirements but I didn't have the money to travel. My wife was in despair. Fortunately, my close friend Albert Ayo, who worked for the government, suggested I contact one of the charity organizations that had been set up to help in this crisis, and the office of the United Nations High Commissioner for Refugees provided the funds. During the ninety-day period, the Ugandan government imposed a curfew for the Asian expatriates; as a result, they had to close their shops in the early afternoon. We had to stay in our houses from seven in the evening till six the next morning. Gunshots were heard every night and I remember seeing dead bodies in the streets.

I can also remember when Idi Amin came into power, on 25 January 1971. General Amin took over Uganda while Milton Obote was temporarily out of the country at a Commonwealth conference. Idi Amin was then the commander-in-chief of the military and he had extensive support from the people. He declared himself the head of state and promised that within the next five years there would be a civilian government. Initially, the civilians were delighted to have Amin as their leader, and he also gained widespread backing from the western world. But not long into his administration, he put a temporary stop to all political movements and civil rights, and his rule became more and more unpredictable.

Even though Amin was under immense pressure to retract the expulsion, he refused to do so. His decision and the atmosphere that had been created drove just about all the Asians to leave, though a few chose to remain. The majority of the Asians went to the United Kingdom; others went to Canada and the United States. The UK stopped all diplomatic relations with Uganda and also imposed a trade embargo, and towards the end of that year, most western countries severed all ties.

I came to England on 26 September 1972. I felt very lucky because I didn't have to stay in a camp; these were old military bases which the government used to provide accommodation for the Asians who didn't have anywhere to live. I went to live with my parents, who already had a house in London. I remember trying so hard to keep my emotions hidden. I felt such a sense of loss because I had had to leave my beloved home, but I also felt a sense of relief that at least I was safe. Landing at Stansted, I couldn't believe that I was actually here in England. I felt a persistent yearning to go back to Uganda, but obviously I couldn't.

I remember walking through the airport and seeing people waving placards in the air with the words: 'Go back to where you come from.' This was not what I had expected, and I was scared of the hostility I was going to face. I was so grateful that my family was in England to give me support, and I felt so much sympathy towards the thousands of other Asians who didn't have that. Charities such as the Red Cross were helping people to settle in the camps and find permanent accommodation in different parts of the UK. The first thing I had to do was to find a job. In Kampala, the capital city of Uganda, I had worked as a cinema projectionist. In London, I found myself a job more or less straight away with an ice-cream company. It was ironic that I came from a hot country and here I was living in a cold country and working in an even colder place. The people I worked with were very friendly and they used to joke: 'If you want to live in England, you'll have to get used to the cold.' They didn't realize that I was in England because I had to be, not because I wanted to be.

I really thought my new life was sorted out, but it's amazing how things change. Two months later, my mother told me in no uncertain terms that I must leave the parental home as soon as I could; she gave me two weeks to find a place to live. I couldn't believe it! There were so many thoughts going through my head. I felt so much sadness and I also felt very alone, but I still had my pride. I found a place to rent in Shepherd's Bush, west London. My wife found it really hard to adjust; she kept on crying and saying that she wanted to go back to Uganda. I used to dream that there would be an announcement on the news that Amin was no longer in power and the Ugandan Asians could return.

The house was damp and cold, but I couldn't complain. I was fortunate to find a house. A lot of landlords didn't want to rent their houses to Ugandan Asians. For a year, I felt content. I had a job and somewhere to live, but, as I mentioned earlier, things change. The ice-cream factory where I was working was closing down and we were all handed our notice. I had a month to find another job. I was applying all the time; on my days off I used to go for two or three interviews at a time, but I wasn't successful. Eventually, I told my family my situation, because I was desperate and they might hear of any jobs available. As a result, I got some good news at last. My elder brother got in touch with me and told me that he was living in a place called Leicester and there was a job as a projectionist at his local cinema. He went on to explain that because Leicester was becoming popular with Asians a local businessman had started showing the latest Indian films. I couldn't believe my luck! The only hitch was that I had to leave London, but I wasn't going to object. I had read about Leicester in the Ugandan press. The city council was discouraging the Asians from settling there and even placed adverts in the Ugandan newspapers stating: 'In your own interests and those of your family, you should accept the advice of the Uganda Resettlement Board and NOT come to Leicester.' When I left Uganda, I had no intention of living there. I thought I was going to settle in London and only moved because of the change in my circumstances. My brother found me somewhere to live that was a two-minute walk from the cinema, in an area called Belgrave.

I thoroughly enjoyed working for the movies again. We showed a film called *Sholay*, which was a very big hit and has since gone down in history as one of the most successful films in Indian cinema. Its popularity was at its peak at this point in 1975, and we would get full houses when this film was running. I made many friends and I even started to frequent the local pub, the Balmoral, which is still there. Even though Leicester had got a reputation as the English city most hostile to the Ugandan Asian refugees, I really enjoyed working and living in the suburbs. My brother gave me a lot of support and helped me adjust to my situation. During this time, more and more Asians were settling in Leicester, especially in Belgrave. Even so, my job came to an end because of a decline in attendance. People were now buying videos so they could watch films in the comfort of their own homes.

My brother came to my rescue again and found me a job at the factory where he worked. For the first time since the ninety-day period, I didn't feel isolated or abandoned, even though I had travelled thousands of miles to the UK. It was the light at the end of a very long and dark tunnel. However, I can still recall the tabloid headlines of that time. The media, it seemed, had taken an instant dislike to the Ugandan Asians. The headlines read: 'New flood of Asians to Britain', 'Another 20,000 Asians are on the way', 'Asians fly out of "New Uganda"' and 'Enough of Asian influx' – just a few of the vast number of unnerving statements that appeared in the newspapers on a daily basis. There were so many times when I thought of Uganda. I missed the country so much. I missed the weather, the food and the beautiful sun-drenched landscape. The reality was that now I was living in Concrete City, surrounded by an icy chilled wind.

I lived as simply as I could. England was my home now and life went on. I didn't feel too isolated with so many Asians living in Belgrave. The Balmoral was a predominantly Asian pub and I knew Ugandan Asians who were living in different parts of Leicester. When I listened to their stories of racial abuse, I was glad that I was living in Belgrave, though I did experience a great deal of abuse myself. The few times I went to other pubs to have a drink, there would always be trouble due to somebody making a comment. I witnessed people having glasses smashed in their faces, getting stabbed and generally being harassed. This put me off going out to pubs and I only went to the Balmoral occasionally. Racism was on the rise, with political parties such as the National Front growing. The local newspaper, the *Leicester Mercury*, was highlighting the arrival of Ugandan Asians, which stirred up prejudice among the people. The unions at companies such as Imperial Typewriters and British Shoe had no regard for the Asian employees and sided with the management. At one stage, Asian workers walked out of Imperial Typewriters because of racist practices at work.

My job at the factory was secure. I used to walk to work and back every day. I worked six days a week and sometimes on a Sunday, when I had the chance to do some overtime. My wife was pregnant so we decided to move house. The bank approved a mortgage and we moved into the house that my wife had her heart set on. I felt as though a big weight was off my shoulders and I could smile again. My daughters started school, and for the first time since leaving Uganda, I felt I had some stability in my life. My son was born in 1977 and I was a very happy man. The only downside was the racial tension growing in Leicester.

It was impossible to ignore and seemed to be getting worse. I'll never forget seeing rival gangs on opposite pavements. I remember walking through the streets of Leicester and seeing National Front slogans and racist graffiti written on the walls, all aimed at Asians. The letters 'KBW' were scrawled in many places; I was told that this stood for 'Keep Britain White'. I really didn't understand why so many people were against the Ugandan Asians. We hadn't wanted to come here in the first place. I felt that the national press enjoyed slating the Asians. Several politicians stated in the newspapers that India had more of an obligation to Ugandan Asians than the UK. At times like these, I used to wish I were back in Uganda. I didn't want to be a burden to this country, and I'm certain other Ugandan Asians felt as I did.

One incident always stays with me: it was Diwali, a Hindu celebration, and I posted a Diwali card to my neighbour. A couple of hours later, he knocked on my door and said he didn't want it. I didn't realize I would offend him, I thought I was being friendly. Years later, we became the best of friends and he apologized for that incident.

I socialized in pubs that I was familiar with in the Belgrave area. The Balmoral had actually been targeted by the National Front. During the mid to late 1970s, the NF became increasingly popular and gained a lot of followers. In Leicester alone, they secured nearly fifteen thousand votes in May 1976, but at the same time, small local committees were forming to oppose the NF ideologies. I remember there were protests against the NF in London, Bradford and other places. In September 1976, an anti-racist campaign was set up, Rock Against Racism. I knew a few people who went to a massive concert they did in Victoria Park, in London, in April 1978, where famous bands such as The Clash, Steel Pulse, X-Ray Spex and the Tom Robinson Band played. I went to see Rock Against Racism when they performed at Leicester Polytechnic in October of that same year. I never could and still don't understand why racism exists. How can you hate someone because of the colour of his or her skin?

In 1979, I read that Idi Amin had launched a military attack on neighbouring Tanzania, but Amin's troops were no match for the Tanzanian Army and Amin and his forces fled, causing devastation along the way. Amin couldn't go back to Uganda so he went into exile in Libya. I also read that he hadn't done Uganda any favours by expelling the Asians. The once-Asian-owned businesses collapsed, and so did the economy. During Amin's regime, Uganda's water supply, schools, hospitals and roads gradually disintegrated. He left the country in total disarray. I felt such sorrow knowing this, for the people left there to pick up the pieces, especially the ones who had lived there for a long time. To witness such a beautiful country being destroyed must have been heartbreaking. In a strange way, I was glad I hadn't been there to see it.

In the same year, the National Front split into smaller factions, but it didn't disappear. Racism was still rife and I experienced lots of racial abuse. People would shout obscenities at me, all aimed at the colour of my skin, as I walked down the street. I was even threatened on a few occasions but I never reacted, it wasn't worth the aggravation. In 1980, the British Movement party was becoming more active. Former members of the National Front were joining this organization, while anti-racist parties were relaunching to confront them. Violent clashes became common. I witnessed the riot in Leicester in July 1981. I couldn't believe what I was seeing in front of my eyes. It was frightful and horrifying and I never want to see anything like that again. There were disturbances in London, Birmingham and other parts of the UK. The inner cities were the worst affected.

I had made friends with many people from the Afro-Caribbean community. I listened with fascination to stories about their lives in the Caribbean. The place sounded similar to Uganda. My conversations with my pals were always dominated by how much we missed our homes. I'm still in contact with a couple of them. I heard the others went back to the Caribbean.

From 1983 through the later years of the decade, I found racial tension declining – it wasn't as bad as in the 1970s. I think this was because the racist parties got less media coverage than they did when they first started. I also believe it was because the Asian and Afro-Caribbean communities set up their own organizations, such as Asian Youth and the Leicester United Caribbean Association. Asian Youth began in the late 1970s, and by 1981 they were established nationwide. The objective of Asian Youth was not to fight in a violent sense but to fight against racism. LUCA was formed in the early 1970s and the association represented Afro-Caribbeans as an ethnic minority and gave them guidance and support when they needed it.

My children were growing up and it seemed to me that everything started changing very fast. The fashion, hairstyles, music and Leicester itself were rapidly altering. Some of the Asians I knew, not just from Africa but the ones I knew from here, were busy arranging their children's marriages. I never agreed with that and I never forced my children to get married. I used to wear flared trousers with shirts that had wide collars. Now I was seeing people with perms and corduroy trousers. I was never a follower of fashion but in the 1980s I wouldn't dare wear my flares or shirts, and I ended up buying myself new clothes. The 1980s music wasn't my cup of tea. In the

1970s, I had enjoyed bands like ABBA, the Bee Gees, the Jackson Five, Gloria Gaynor, Brotherhood of Man and all the songs from the film *Grease*.

It was quite remarkable for me to watch my children embrace British culture. My daughters wanted freedom to socialize with their friends from college. They used to accuse me of being strict, and I used to tell them I was only concerned for their safety. I didn't mind that they were living the western way of life, but I didn't want any of my children to forget their Indian heritage. Looking back now, I do realize how confusing it must have been for them; it was just as bewildering for me. I particularly missed my parents, brothers and sisters. In Uganda, we had been a close-knit family; it seemed that once we left we separated and went our own ways. I know that we have lost the family bond. I see them at special and religious occasions and we still have conversations, and it is always nice to meet up with them but the closeness is not there.

My life changed in the 1990s. I was made redundant at the factory where I had worked for so many years. I decided to retrain as an electrician, because I was familiar with electrical appliances. I was at college for three years; I got my qualifications and began to apply for jobs. One of my very good friends owned an electrical company and gave me a job – I'm still working for him to this day. My elder daughter went to live abroad, my younger daughter still lives in Leicester with her son and my son went to study in Spain.

I even got a job calling the bingo at the local Working Men's Club. I made a multitude of friends there. I have always been, as they say, 'a people's person'. Leicester was a favourite choice for Asians to live, and there were twice as many Asians now than there had been during the 1970s and 1980s. Numerous Indian restaurants opened, alongside sari, gold and grocery stores. Diwali and other significant festivals respected by different faiths were being celebrated not just in Leicester but all over England. The Working Men's Club even introduced 'Asian nights'. I was glad of the positive progress that is still going on in England. Every now and again, my thoughts went back to Uganda. As time went by, I didn't miss it any less. It's not the country I left, but I still like to think of it as a wonderful place.

Towards the end of the 1990s, I found that everything was getting more and more expensive, from house prices to day-to-day living. I called it the 'computer age', not that I knew how to switch one on, let alone use one! The young people in this country were very lucky to be living here. They had so many opportunities that I never had. My wife used to say that she had always wanted to go to college to study nursing, but she never got the chance. This decade went really fast for me and, before I knew it, the twenty-first century was here. It was twenty-eight years since we arrived. The next six years went by peacefully. I travelled to Las Vegas, Spain and Dubai. Life carried on as normal. Nobody I knew mentioned colour or race, and they were all against racism. I remember watching a video that my friend took of Uganda when he went to visit. The place looked modern and tranquil. It still had breathtaking green scenery – this always sticks in my mind. Halfway through watching, my wife walked out of the room in tears and said she couldn't bear to watch any more. I totally understood why she was so emotional. Entebbe Airport, the same airport we left from, looked like any other airport in the world. I was surprised to hear that many tourists visit Uganda and that Kampala is a very safe city to travel in, the crime rate at an all-time low.

It is now 2007 and I can honestly say that I am very happy to be living in England. I will always hold this country in high regard; it was the country that gave me and thousands of others salvation. The first few years of living here were horrendous, but as time went on things changed for the better. My experiences have taught me that it doesn't matter what colour skin we have, we are all human beings. I educated my children to never discriminate against anyone because of their race and to treat other people as they themselves would want to be treated. I'm proud to say they have listened to this piece of advice.

I have seen many changes in Leicester – not all of them good. I know racism is still widespread but it is not as bad as it used to be. I'm aware of the drink and drug culture, especially among the younger generation. I feel that, on the whole, respect and manners have declined, and I think this has led to an increase in crime. I have seen good changes as well. People are more tolerant to other races. The education system and National Health Service are fantastic and always have been. The benefit and housing systems have improved tremendously. I'm pleased to see so many people in mixed-race relationships.

There will always be a slight emptiness in my heart where Uganda's concerned. It was called 'the pearl of Africa', and to me it was. I'll never forget it as long as I'm alive. The government wants the Asians back, but I will never return. I won't even visit the country because I have too many memories. Sometimes when I'm on my own and I think of my life in Uganda, I can't help but cry. The aching in my heart is still there and I suppose always will be. I often wonder what my children's life would've been like if we were still there. So many people's lives changed on 5 August 1972.

I am indebted to the British government and also to the charities that came to my aid. I am settled in

Leicester and I couldn't be happier. I'm not living in fear and I have freedom. I'm proud to be living in a multicultural city that has so many organizations representing and helping people of different cultures and faiths. The British Asian Uganda Trust is a charity that raises money for British charities as a way of saying 'thank you' to Britain.

My hopes and aspirations for the future are that racism, violence, hate and fear become things of the past. I truly believe that life is for living and being happy. We should all be able to live in peace and harmony.

# I Love My Neighbours

*Zlatko Pranjic*

'London is a great city, Zed. So far away from the trouble one can get in a country like Yugoslavia. Why don't you forget the past, once and for all, and start a new life? After all, that's why you are here,' says my friend Ivan, rolling his eyes upwards as if he were speaking some obvious truth that only I can't see. In our friendship, he is the grown-up, and has always been, ever since we met at the grammar school in Zenica, the industrial town in central Bosnia where we were born. He loves his London life, but he strongly believes that I am not happy here. Well, he is right about that: I am not, although it has nothing to do with where I live or what I do.

'There is no such thing,' I reply lethargically.

'There is no such what?'

'There is no Yugoslavia; consequently there is no trouble in Yugoslavia. What you mean is that trouble started once Yugoslavia was cut into pieces.' I try to be sarcastic.

'Oh, don't start. It was not meant to be. Yugoslavia was a big historical mistake . . .'

'Fuck off, Ivo. Go on, recite nonsense slogans, hand in hand with the bloody nationalists.'

'You see, there is no way one can talk to you, because you never give credit to anybody's opinion but your own; that's an attitude inherited from your communist upbringing.'

As if to confirm it, I shower him with beer and leave the pub, ashamed. I lost it again. I can't keep it cool like all these smart people around us whose troubles have never involved anything as impersonal as politics. I love Ivan. I love London and its values, but who would trust me now, after this?

Summer 1993:
*The hunting season on Bosnians in Croatia had reached its peak. War between yesterday's allies, the Croats and Muslims in Bosnia, had broken out again. My family name, stigmatized months earlier when this territory was Muslim-controlled, now sounded less alien to a Croatian nationalist's ear, as my grandfather and many others with that name died fighting with Croatian Ustaše, in alliance with Hitler, for the independent Croatia cleansed of Serbs, Gypsies and Jews. Luckily, my Serbian mother, whose father heroically fought fascists in the Big War, and my love for the cause could not be read on my forehead.*

It was six o'clock in the morning when our bus entered the suburbs of Zagreb, Croatia's capital, on the first day of August. I instinctively woke and jumped up from my seat. Convincing the driver to let me off before we reached the city's main bus station, one of the favourite hunting spots for the police, did not take long and I was out, in a fresh summer morning, after forty-eight hours of intense struggle to regain my freedom.

Two days earlier, during a police sweep, I had been arrested for failing to produce Croatian ID. The police had set a trap a few yards from the editorial office of a magazine I occasionally worked for.

Early citizens were passing by in a hurry, their eyes pinned on the pavement as if they wanted to keep their thoughts hidden from intruders. I arrived with a friend, S.S., another journalist, who had picked me up from my aunt's house. He drove and talked that morning just like any other day: about Milosevic being Tudjman's brother in their bloody politics; about a bridge Tudjman had opened under silent Serbian artillery; about everything. He talked a bit too much. When we arrived, he parked his car in front of the coffee shop across the road from our office and invited me for a coffee.

'Thanks, I already had one. I have to finish my article,' I replied ill-temperedly.

'Oh, come on!' he insisted.

We entered the coffee shop and I went straight towards the toilets. I noticed an odd silence inside the main room but did not pay much attention to it.

While I washed my hands, a man came in. Another followed. Dressed inappropriately for a hot summer morning, in black leather jackets, the two men looked like Bosnian unskilled workers. Their pale wrinkled faces revealed an unhealthy lifestyle. An odour of garlic and smoked bacon spread around them.

'We are the police! Show us your ID!' the first shouted out.

'Yeah, right,' I answered, acknowledging the joke. As I tried to walk out, their two heavy bodies blocked the door.

I had been detained by various police units and paramilitaries on previous occasions during the war, and I had been threatened several times with being shot for a wrong word or for the music of my name, but never before had I felt such devastating claustrophobia as at that moment, in the toilet of the smoky coffee shop. Once triggered, this feeling influenced my life, accompanied by paranoia – a fear that I am being followed, usually by Croatian and Bosnian radical nationalists who still hold important positions in the new governments of the former Yugoslavian republics, particularly in their secret services.

Winter 2006–7:
Sitting with Duda in a local pub in Portobello Road, I notice a parked car outside, its driver looking at me.

'Can you see that man, the one sitting in that car?

I saw him, I swear I saw him in front of the embassy on the night my film was premièred,' I whisper frantically into Duda's ear.

'Calm down. I am sure you've mistaken him for the other man. Nobody is following you, there is no reason. You are in London now.' She strokes my shoulder.

'Really? So I am imagining it, am I?'

'Zed, you are.'

'Okay, if I *am* mad, goodbye then. Go and find somebody who isn't. Just one question before I go. Do you remember my friend R.M., who left Zagreb a few hours after I was arrested in 1993 and then went back eleven years later? He was found hanged in his apartment in Zagreb. We were both part of the Anti-War Campaign group, and before he left Croatia, he wrote about war crimes committed by Croatian paramilitaries. What about M.B., who died mysteriously of an overdose at the moment he was about to publish some damaging revelations about the government's involvement in –'

'ZED, JUST STOP IT, PLEASE! It's over. You don't have to go there ever again. R.M. hanged himself because he was suffering from depression. All your friends who saw him said he was run down.'

'I am depressed myself. So if you find me hanging from a ceiling one day, will you simply accept that I hanged myself?'

I leave the pub, thinking of my psychiatrist's advice not to try too hard. On the other hand, my Jungian psychotherapist suggested I should go for it, try to understand my past in order to free myself from the fear. The man in the car, outside the pub, has mysteriously disappeared. Duda stays behind, crying.

Summer 1993:
Edin T. worked at the offices of the Croatian Anti-War Campaign on Tkalciceva Street, and that summer morning in 1993 I knew I could trust him. He lived in a small flat, on a passage off the main road, with his girlfriend, Milena, another human rights activist from Zagreb.

(When I bumped into Edin on the same streets twelve years later, he was a bitter man: working as head of Amnesty International in the area, still raging about the current conduct of the Croatian government, its constant breaching of human rights, the corruption of individuals and state. About the CIA following him. Tired from fighting windmills, visibly disturbed.)

Edin shook his head in disbelief, as if he was seeing a ghost. He had heard of my arrest from another journalist, but he did not know what exactly had happened to me afterwards. He acted fast. In a few hours, I became a protégé of the Office of the United Nations High Commissioner for Refugees.

It took some time for me to understand the inevitable: I had to go if I wanted to breathe. Since leaving prison, I hadn't slept in the same bed twice; I kept moving from place to place, instinctively avoiding journalist friends, trusting female colleagues only. I was not the first to be taken care of by pragmatic women during those days of dangerous living, while many men betrayed their close friends for patriotic or professional or other reasons. This 'politically incorrect' statement is a very true one. Finally, I had no choice but to go.

'Don't worry, you will be safe in England,' Marco R., the UNHCR official, comforted me. 'The English will take care of you until all this is sorted out. One day, you will come back, or you may stay – who knows?'

Winter 2006–7:
I live in London, somewhere between Notting Hill and Camden Town. After almost fourteen years living in the UK, I am no longer who I was. No surprise. Or maybe I only wish something had changed. There are so many aspects of me that can't be altered.

For instance, I still write whenever my fragile health allows me to. I occasionally go to see my friends, or they visit me in my council flat. My friends come from all over the world, bringing in their veins a part of their own soil, creating a mixture known as London's cosmopolitan scene.

Sotiris is a Greek whose first wife, Lena, comes from Lebanon. Their daughter, Anastasia, is a fourteen-year-old polyglot who speaks perfect French, Arabic, Greek and English. Sotiris lives with his second wife, Nilam, a Canadian of Punjabi origin, with two daughters, Leka and Ariadni, who learn their first words in the tiny kitchen of a council flat. Sotiris, who has a PhD from Westminster University, works part-time as a builder.

Paul is a fifty-year-old British man whose Indian father met his Jewish mother in Manchester after her dramatic escape from Berlin during the Second World War. Paul is a writer who spends a lot of his free time with my friends from former Yugoslavia, astonished by their passionate, loud arguments (in our language, whatever you want to call it: Serbo-Croatian, Serbian, Croatian or Bosnian) about football, literature, theatre, politics, love and hate, anything really. He picks out the most dramatic words and wants to learn them.

Irina is a Bulgarian fairy. She works as a living statue in Covent Garden.

William is an energetic Englishman whose age is unknown (between forty and sixty). He works with disabled people and brings us all together at charity events, festivals, parties, weddings and funerals.

Paula is an Italian. She works for the fashion industry. Xavier is a Spanish poet who does not work. Celine is French and travels around the world. Nadia and Farah are Palestinian refugees. Dado is a composer from Bosnia. Mark is a British-Caribbean musician, et cetera, et cetera, et cetera.

I wonder to what extent this city has altered me. One could argue that in fourteen years I would have changed regardless of the circumstances, due to the ageing phenomenon. One thing that will always be the same is my family. After so many years together, we are still inarticulate.

My sister, Zeljka, lives in Derby. She is a successful professional working for Rolls-Royce, while her husband, Samir, teaches information technology at the local college. They speak English only at their work. Anja and Anel, their children (both born in Bosnia), never speak in their mother tongue. My parents, Ilija and Zivana, live in Derby too. They never speak in English. Together we are the embodiment of a nationalist's nightmare. Muslim, Christian Orthodox and Catholic culture are all in our 'atheist genes'. Romanian, Serbian, Croatian, Bosnian, Turkish are just a few predecessors we 'remember' with certainty. And countless, brutal wars.

21 September 1993:
Early morning. I said goodbye to a couple of friends, journalists for an independent radio station in the city, whose hospitality, among others', helped me keep a low profile after my escape.

J.P. took me to the city airport. I watched Zagreb through the windscreen of her car and thought of my family: my parents, my sister and her baby children left behind, in the war zone of Bosnia. I had not spoken to them for six months, as telephone lines were disconnected. J.P. guessed my thoughts. She started a conversation about her friend, a British war reporter, asking whether I remembered him. He is the one with that funny hairstyle. Yes, I do. She found out that morning that he is going back to central Bosnia and would not mind taking a small parcel with him. She will send some food for my family, and some money, but I need to write down their address. There is no time to write a long letter, but I should think fast: here is a piece of paper.

> *My dear . . .*
> *I hope this letter finds you all well . . . I am alive and fat –*
> *don't worry for me, Mum. Dad, take care of everybody. I*
> *hope this parcel will help you to feed the kids for a*
> *while. I must leave the country but I am OK. I have a*
> *British visa and the British Red Cross will take proper*
> *care of me. I love you all . . . Have to run . . . Z.*

In the airport I joined a small group of traditionally dressed Muslim women, accompanied by several exhausted-looking men ruled by fear. There was noticeable unrest in their eyes. Marco R. stood in the middle, explaining the airport procedure through a translator. I found out later about these men: they were Muslims, mainly survivors from various concentration camps run by either Serbian or Croatian paramilitary units across Bosnia and Herzegovina. A few steps away, a Croatian policeman quietly examined our faces, as if looking for someone. I dropped my bag on the floor and withdrew from the group, squeezing J.P.'s hand in panic.

'What if they are looking for me? I think they are. They will never let me go; they are afraid I may tell my story abroad,' I whispered to my friend.

'Don't panic now,' she responded calmly. 'Everything will be fine, trust me, and they would not know who is on the UNHCR list.'

'Still, they are looking for me. For almost two months, I never slept in the same place, I lived the life of a shadow. I could smell the secret police miles away, but now I am visible.'

'Stop please,' she begged me.

We spent ten minutes talking nervously about anything that crossed our minds: our friendship, the end of summer, the English weather . . .

'MR ZED IS REQUESTED TO COME IMMEDIATELY TO DEPARTURES . . .'

'It is over,' I cried. 'They have got me now.'

'Don't . . . just go.'

Standing over my luggage, with his legs spread and

his arms behind his back, a policeman looked at me irritably. My group had already left. It seemed, at that moment, that I was not going to join them.

'Is this your luggage?' asked the policeman in a firm voice.

'Yes, it is. Why?' I answered, confused and frightened.

'Why? Is that your answer? There could be a bomb in there. You are not supposed to leave your bag like this in an airport.'

'Sorry, sir.' Marco R. came to my rescue. 'He is with me. Follow me!' he ordered, and I followed obediently.

An aeroplane rolled up the runway, took off and then flew to freedom!

Life in England has never been as smooth and easy as I imagined it would be on 21 September 1993, while riding clouds above the old continent. When the UNHCR, in cooperation with the British Home Office, fulfilled another promise and evacuated the rest of my family a year later, to reunite them with me, I thought – this is it! I can relax, for the worst has been put behind me and my closest ones are alive.

I still remember, vividly, the horror of the war. Whenever I see the ugly face of hate and ignorance, I remember; when I hear a dumb nationalist scream-ing on the television, here or there, I remember; when

I go back to an ex-Yugoslavian country where the border guard, often, is *one of them*, knowing from his screen that I am not (*one of them*), I remember . . .

Maybe I should listen to Ivan, my grown-up friend, and forget the countries which once were my home. Maybe I should never go there again. I should turn around instead and love my neighbours. They live their quiet life with such dignity. When they, for some trivial reason, get loud – because the sun is shining or the husband and father has brought in shopping bags full of family happiness – I spy through my curtains.

I think that my neighbours come from Iran, maybe Syria or Iraq. I have wanted to ask them for years where they come from, but I am shy in front of these proud people.

I remember when I came to the neighbourhood, five years ago, they were whispering in their mysterious language, perhaps asking one another who I am, where do I come from, am I a good or a bad man, do I live quietly or am I going to be the one who annoys them with loud music and frequent parties?

For a while, I really annoyed them – I listened to loud music, my intrusive friends shouted their politics, passionately, late into the night – but they never complained.

# Albert Finney's Smile

*Nimer Rashed*

*I'm out for a good time – all the rest is propaganda!*
  – Arthur Seaton

Years ago, in a darkened room, my dad watched Albert Finney smile. As Arthur Seaton in *Saturday Night and Sunday Morning*, Finney brawled his way across the screen with a fag perched on his lips, a frown across his forehead and cufflinks that shone like shrapnel. He was mesmerizing.

Finney was a great actor, but there was more to it than that. As my father watched him thunder, a smile broke out. Ask him now and he'll say there was no light bulb. No moment of epiphany. There was Albert Finney tearing through the streets, out for a good time on the beer and stout. Albert Finney out for a good time – and that, to him, meant freedom.

When he arrived at Heathrow Airport on April Fools' Day 1971, my dad's freshly polished shoes met the tarmac with a squeak. The sky was a dull, cloudless grey. The air hostesses wore blue. He was twenty-two years old. The man at immigration, mustachioed and brisk, asked why he was here.

'I am sorry,' my dad said, enunciating each syllable as carefully as his Berlitz guide had suggested. 'Could you repeat that, please?'

'What's the purpose of your visit?' said the man in a monotone. Then, seeing my dad was at a loss, he spoke more slowly.

'Why are you here?'

The question took a moment to sink in. Realizing that this was not an existential query and that he was not, in fact, required to negotiate his way through the precepts of ontology and the Kantian metaphysics of morals with his limited English, my father gave his answer with no little relief.

'I want to be an actor,' he said.

And it was true. Back home in Haifa, he'd been given a generous bursary allowing him to leave Israel and study acting overseas. The award, no mean feat, had even merited a mention in *Time*. And here he was in London, following in the steps of Finney, Harris, O'Toole and Burton. Anything was possible, nothing was forbidden. As he received the stamp in his passport, he shook the immigration man by the hand and kissed him on the cheek. 'Thank you,' said my father. 'Thank you very much.' The man's moustache bristled at the impertinence. 'Next,' he said. My dad moved on.

When I try to picture London in the 1970s, I see long hair, flares, and Routemaster buses whistling through the streets – buses managed by bright-eyed conductors with ruddy cheeks winking knowingly at comely matrons hauling bags of petticoats to wash-rooms in the Old Kent Road. I'm told it wasn't quite like that, but not so far from it either.

'It was the New World,' my father says. 'Everything was so innocent. You'd walk down the road and in half the windscreens there'd be signs saying, "Tax disc in post." It was crazy.'

My dad revelled in this idyll, not quite believing his luck. Some habits remained: for years he carried his passport with him wherever he went. Eventually someone asked the obvious question. My father laughed, then looked more serious. 'But what if someone stops me?'

At first, I thought these words said a lot about the fear he'd experienced in his early years in England, but I was wrong – he'd been stung by prejudice long before he arrived. Growing up in Haifa, my father was labelled an Arab-Israeli. To this day, he stays away from hyphens. This toothpick splinter did little to bridge the chasm. It was a Band-Aid applied to a split jugular, and those branded with the telltale splice, the plaster across their throats, have not found their lives easy.

Imagine, then, the joy of arriving in 1970s London.

Today, the would-be asylum seeker is met with fear and misunderstanding, headlines that shriek in bold sans serif print. My dad was greeted with peace signs, Volkswagens and dope-addled men called Steve. Buoyed with confidence, flicking his newly purchased flared trousers round corner after corner with swishes of glee, he made his way, clutching a photocopied monologue from *Orestes*, to London's Drama Centre, where he took a deep breath and spoke passionately of the death of Clytemnestra. The judges were impressed. For the first time, history didn't matter, borders weren't a problem and hyphens didn't get in the way. His passion had spoken for itself, and he was awarded a place at the school.

'London was so English then,' he says, unwittingly echoing the manifesto of the BNP. 'Everything was English. Telephone boxes, ounces, shillings – everything was different, unique. These days we're reaching out towards Europe – even the buses are like Germany. So Englishness is disappearing.'

I get it, but it's not really something I can understand. My mind reaches for images of what he's talking about, but all I see are David Tomlinson and Angela Lansbury in *Bedknobs and Broomsticks*. Is this what was lost? Bowler hats and umbrellas bobbing along at the bottom of the sea? The London I've grown up with is so far from the one my father remembers that my attempt to visualize it is a foolish, dizzy amalgam of images, history as a series of half-reels, in which Leonard Rossiter melts into Monty Python, *Blowup* cross-fades into *One of Our Dinosaurs Is Missing*, all spliced together in a messy blur of which, one suspects, Eisenstein would not be proud.

Not so my father. For him, recalling the early years brings a sense of calm. You can feel the click and whirr as memories are slotted into the gate. You can hear the hum of the projection bulb being switched on, see the light come into his eyes. The men from the BNP, as they scrawl their midnight manifestos in their Devon taverns, might be surprised to learn they're not the only ones who're aching with nostalgia. My father, now in his fifties, looks back at the highlights reel with no less fondness.

'I'm a sucker for it all,' he says. 'I found it so romantic, this Englishness. For some reason, I still hanker for it. When I retire, all I want – all I've ever wanted – is a small cottage in the countryside with books, bottles of wine. That, to me, is England.'

When my father speaks like this, my mother rolls her eyes. And yet he's not the only one who's seduced by this vision of Albion. The dream the BNP is fighting to protect is the same dream so many people come here for, the myth of Englishness that still pervades the world, as it pervades my father's fantasies. If life is lived in one direction, a linear progression, this reverie of what once was, of what could be, is a step over this experiential line into the white space that lies beyond. It is the awful daring of a moment's surrender. It is the desire to think, and live, outside the box.

So when my father tells me that the 1970s were a simpler time, I like to think it's true. I like to believe that the Volkswagens tooted and the flares were hip. I like all the old stories, and so does he.

As my father has gone on to build an acting career over the last thirty-odd years, his list of credits reveals a great deal about this country's relationship with his part of the world. In addition to the standard roles – waiters, café owners, misanthropes – he's played men on camels and oil-rich sheikhs more times than he can remember. In the 1970s, he started off as a junior terrorist. He soon moved up to the role of ambassador; last year he played al-Qaeda kingpin Ayman al-Zawahiri. My father accepts these roles with a weary shrug. These weren't the parts he dreamed of, but he's used to it. He's been a terrorist all his life.

Immigration is a big word. It implies journeys, boundaries, distance, breadth. It inspires fear in some, hope in others. But like the hyphen between the two halves of my father's identity, it doesn't really mean anything by itself. Everyone comes from somewhere. We are all immigrants – it's just that some of us inherit our passports while others fight for them. The story of immigration is thus the story of survival, the ebbs and flows of humanity across a segregated planet.

My father fought hard to get a British passport. He likens the struggle to the climb up a ladder embedded in quicksand. Now that he has it, it's not what he expected.

'The value of things erodes with time. You reach for the passport, you get it, but by then it's worthless. It's not what you aspired to.'

I find it hard to agree with this. It's doubtless true that once you reach the mountaintop the view's not always what you expected, but as I sit writing this I look outside and see a different London from the one he grew up in – one with steeper ridges, deeper gorges and many mountains left to climb. I see them because of his adventures, his fight with the Home Office, his struggle to stay on. We don't often say anything, but all of us – the British Asians, BBCs, the half-bred, mixed-up mongrel lot of us – feel the same way.

Sometimes as I look up high into the hills, wondering what adventures will be next, I see an old man looking down. He holds a white cane and a battered, blood-red passport in his outstretched hand. I can just make out the grin upon his face. It's just like Albert Finney's.

# How We are Haunted

*Anita Sethi*

'I'm turning into my mother,' she sighed, as she peered at the ghost staring out from the dark-green Guyanan passport which lived beneath layers of dust and cobwebs and old letters and jewellery at the bottom of her wardrobe in Old Trafford, Manchester.

'Do you think I look like her?' she asked, gazing into the mirror, pulling at her flesh and making funny faces.

As two-dimensional as the passport picture was the map of the world Blu-Tacked to the wall of my bedroom. A blue biro line cut through Guyana, the 'Land of Many Waters', bordered by Suriname, Brazil and Venezuela in South America. All of the Guianas reach out towards the Atlantic Ocean, reaching out to the Caribbean Islands, reaching further out to North America, to England, to India. Another blue biro line cut around England, and another around Kenya, where Dad was born. Roots are as tangled as seaweed, wrapping around each other, and when storms come, they tighten their grip on each other, pulling, pushing, trying to ebb and flow at the same time – the Caribbean, the Indian, the British jostling for control. Mum left for England when she was twenty-one years old, in 1969, after British Guiana broke away into independence. Dad, too, left Kenya when the country gained independence.

I took my first step in Guyana, aged one. It is one of those memories that I am not really sure of; perhaps it is just a photograph come to life, coloured to such intensity that story and life blur, their edges melting into each other. We were staying at Wellington Aunty's house, so called because she lived in Wellington (named after the Duke when the British arrived and set up shop). There were so many aunties that the only way to distinguish them was to name them after their place or trade.

That first step was shaky, stumbling upon a world whose boundaries were unknown. And yet traversing history is as uncertain still as that early ground beneath my feet; I never do know when the earth will give way to a huge crater, a sudden hole beneath me where there is no knowledge, when I will get lost all of a sudden with no arrows or signposts to point me in the right direction.

Although Mum knows that her ancestors were originally from India, she is not quite sure which generation or which part of India. And so there's a blank patch in my history, as if someone has burnt away a portion of memory, a blind spot where knowledge vanishes. History and fiction blur as she seems to make things up: one time we are from Calcutta, another from Agra. So we just do not know.

Imagination, then, is called on to play its part in the immigrant tale (although my mother does not like to be referred to as an 'immigrant'; the word sounds so negative in the current climate, she says, and she would rather be known as a 'migrant'). I have trawled through what facts I know, shoring them up like pebbles on a beach, hard and tangible gifts. That is why my experience, as the daughter of two immigrants born on opposite sides of the globe, South America and Africa, pushes geographical boundaries and also pushes the boundaries of narrative forms. Its fractured nature seeks containment in the page, its sure edges, its black-and-whiteness, its finite word limit, as it at once wriggles out of those confining boundaries.

There are ghosts on the other side of the family too, in a corner shop which curves around a road of Old Trafford, this rainy town, opposite the Lancashire Cricket Ground. The shop is shuttered up now, since Mama died. We are going up to my father's mother's bedroom, past the living room with its brown furry carpet and the photograph of her husband, framed and gazing out on to her emptiness, past the cupboard which stored old dolls the grandchildren had outgrown, up into the attic at the top, which we are sure is haunted. I am sure it is haunted, that I felt her presence, heard something move in the dark, musty-smelling room with a picture of her on the side table and a copy of the *Mahabharata* in Hindi on the bedside table.

The room grows chilly and black rain begins to cover the city again.

'From where do you belong?' asks the cashier in the supermarket, a question thrown out innocently enough, but the answer is too convoluted to give quickly, in the time it takes to put the bananas and apples into the bag. History will ooze through clear-cut boundaries and boxes; I come to fill out the application form for this competition and my hand hovers over the boxes, unsure of where to place myself, whether I am British Asian Indian or whether I am Other.

'From where do I belong?' has no single answer; it shifts and changes as I am asked to tell people my name. I pronounce my surname differently; some-times I say it softly, my tongue crushed against the back of my teeth so that the 't' is soft, Anglicized, the way my mother says it. Other times I roll the vowel in the word out and push my tongue to the roof of my mouth so you can hear the 't', the way my father says it and the way it is said in India, so that my name trips out of my mouth and into the world sounding like a different name entirely. But sometimes I open my mouth to say my name and the two ways of being clash against each other, the soft and hard sounds, the open and closed, and what comes out is muffled, discordant. I stumble over my own name, clumsily, like a child taking its first steps through language, unsure yet of the boundaries of their world, physically or linguistically, and I am asked to repeat myself, so I have to start all over again with that tricky business of saying my name. I have to choose which identity to imbue into the sound, which ghosts I shall allow to haunt me.

# Out of Germany

*Xenia Crockett*

The long train rattled across the Kentish countryside towards London on a dark, wet and cold evening. I peered out of the dirty, smeared window. So this is England. All the houses have washing hanging in their back gardens – at home that would not be allowed; they have strictly regulated times when it is permitted to hang washing outside. It is 30 December 1949 and I am three weeks short of my sixteenth birthday. This is the first hour of my new life in this strange country. Did I want to come here? Was I not happy where I was before, at home in post-war Germany? For a moment, I forget the rotten, hurtful life we'd led there – never belonging, always being picked on. I peer outside again; the scenery has not changed. We stop at dimly lit stations. Stationmasters blow their whistles and wave their flags. At least that is the same as home. The train rattles on.

'Come and sit down,' says Nadia, my older sister. 'It's not long now. It'll be better when we see Papa.'

Our father had became stateless when he left his homeland, Russia, after the revolution. He settled in Germany when he married our mother, who then also became stateless. It followed that their seven children were born stateless too. He was allowed into England in 1946 and from London organized the emigration of his family from Germany.

Nadia and I are the second contingent to join him; two older sisters, Elena (known as Mausi) and Mariamna, and our only brother, Victor, had been allowed into England about a year earlier. And when the Home Office quota next allowed, our mother and two remaining sisters, Olga and Vera, will join us.

In 1921, the Council of the League of Nations asked that great humanitarian Fridtjof Nansen to administer its High Commission for Refugees. For the stateless refugees under his care he invented the 'Nansen passport', a document of identification which was eventually recognized by fifty-two governments. We had been issued with Nansen passports by the Allied Occupational Forces which would allow us to move out of Germany.

After an emotional farewell at Wiesbaden Hauptbahnhof, Nadia and I climb aboard the big, black train with two suitcases. One holds all I possess: some clothes, my precious stamp album and postcards from my penfriends in the USA. We wave to our mother and slowly, hissing white steam, the train chugs out of the station. We settle into our seats. I have no idea what is waiting for me in that strange country I know only from my few English lessons. One teacher had said, 'It always rains in England and if it does not rain, it is foggy.' Life may be easier and freer, there may be less being picked on and laughed at. London is supposed to be very big. Nobody will know me, and nobody will be able to pick me out as being different – perhaps.

The train stops a few times on its way along the Rhine towards Belgium and Ostend, where we'll cross the English Channel to Dover. Night descends. The train halts at the Belgian border as morning breaks grey on the far horizon. It's not a proper station. There's shouting outside. Police and soldiers run around. Somebody opens a carriage door and shouts, 'All Germans out.'

'Are we Germans?' I ask Nadia. She doesn't know. The passport control personnel moving through the train glance at our passports and wave us out of the carriage. We have to drag our cases with us. There are long queues, many questions for people. Suitcases and bags are opened and rummaged through. When our turn comes, nobody is sure what to make of us. We are waved away and drag ourselves and our cases back on to the train. In time, it pulls away from the customs place and we continue towards Ostend, the Channel and, eventually, England.

I have a fear of water. I have not given a thought to crossing the Channel and floating in a boat across the deep water until we troop from the train to the boat. But I have to face it. 'I will cross it once and, if I arrive alive, I will not cross it again. I will stay in that country where it always rains,' I promise myself.

On board, it is windy and cold. A wet mist drifts around. We find a couple of deckchairs and Nadia orders some tea. A tray arrives with two cups of hot water, each dangling a Lipton's teabag. This is something new and it tastes delicious. An elderly lady sits with us and after a little chat in broken German, she produces a hip flask and offers us both a small sip 'to warm us up'. This is my first taste of alcohol – to this day cognac is my favourite. I still remember how it burnt my throat that first time. Some hours later, we arrive in Dover and troop on to another train. It is getting dark again. We should arrive in London around seven o'clock.

The train pulls into a very long station. Like the others, it is dimly lit. Many people are waiting. Surprisingly, we spot Papa, our two sisters and brother, who have come to meet us here at Victoria Station in the heart of London. We fall into each other's arms and don't know whether to cry or laugh. Lots of people are pushing and shoving, shouting, laughing and even crying. Papa bundles us all into a huge, black car, a hackney carriage, as ubiquitous in London as cockles and mussels are in the East End. I learn that not only does it always rain in this country but they also drive on the opposite side of the road. I cower in the corner of the taxi and prepare for a future consisting of my worst fears.

Our new home is the basement of a large terraced house in Kensington. On the ground floor are a large entrance hall and the house chapel, with stairs leading to the upper floors. On the next floor are the kitchen, a large dining room and a study/bedroom for the priest. On the halfway landing is a spare room where Nadia will sleep, and on the top floor are two more rooms.

In the basement we have a small toilet, a cabinet which contains a bathtub, and two rooms separated by a folding partition, which allows the area to open out to be used for parish functions, plus a corner which serves as kitchen. My heart sinks – this is what I have come here for? What we have all come here for? Our evacuee accommodation during the war in Michaelsbach now seems like a palace in comparison. Nobody says anything. Papa is happy to have more of his family with him. After a meal, we all find somewhere to sleep.

Next day, we have to formalize our existence in England. First call is Kensington Town Hall for our ration books. Ration books? This seems odd, as a few days before we left Germany all rationing had ceased. We are interviewed and have to produce our papers, passports and entry permits with length of permitted stay. I understand very little. My English appears to be Americanized and it all sounds so different.

Clutching our precious ration books, we catch a bus to Piccadilly to a department connected with the Home Office. I had heard of Piccadilly in my English lessons. I am beginning to feel more at home and, better yet, it is not raining. Here we are interviewed by the police. I am young enough to be allowed in as a minor. Nadia has a visitor's visa which she can extend or exchange for a permit to stay, which she opts for in the end. We are provided with Aliens Certificates of Registration in exchange for our passports. These we have to carry with us at all times and show when required. We are told they have to be renewed from time to time but they establish our right to be and live in England. I begin to feel a little less stateless. I have been very quiet all day. Used to being the star in our class in Germany, I soon realize that my schoolgirl English is sadly lacking. Nadia and I have to register with a doctor. We have arrived in the land of the National Health Service, which is the envy of many countries. We complete forms and are sent for chest X-rays, which are returned clear, and after a few weeks we receive our National Health cards, which we have to always carry with us.

Back in our basement home, we settle down. Nadia, who still thinks of perhaps going back to Germany, does the tourist thing and drags me along. We see as much of London as we can: the Tower; the Changing of the Guard; Westminster Abbey; the Houses of Parliament; St Paul's Cathedral; and, for some reason, Gamages, a huge department store in Holborn. Nadia knows of all the places that have to be seen.

I am asked what I want to do, the choices being: full-time schooling, doing an intensive English-for-foreigners course with a Royal Society of Arts examination at the end, or going out to work. Papa enrols me for the class. Each morning, I catch the Tube from Holland Park to Warren Street, changing at Tottenham Court Road. I go back home for lunch and then repeat the morning's journey. Walking to and from the station, I study the shop fronts. There are several car showrooms, which are of little interest to me, but the front of the Esperanto Language School is especially interesting: many colourful placards posted on the walls and several desks placed in the centre, but remarkable in that it always seems to be empty. At the station and on the Tube I read all the adverts. Everything is so new to me.

School is a real eye-opener. There are many nationalities of all ages. The teacher, a short, little man, introduces himself as a bachelor and juggles his diverse students along to the required standard. Many just pass through: after two or three weeks they don't come back. My best memory of him is talking about politics and once being asked what 'MP' stood for. Quick as lightning I volunteer, 'Military Police.' He looks at me and says jovially, 'Yes, but here we call them Members of Parliament.' Apart from politics, he loves to talk about cooking. From him I get a tip about always washing your hands with cold water after peeling onions, so as not to open the pores and let the onion smell in. I learn that English people have a 'thing' about onions and garlic.

In due course, May comes, I sit my exam and promptly forget about the course. I am learning English in all areas of my life. Next door lives a family with a young grandson, Nicky. I am asked if I'd like to babysit for them, which really means taking Nicky for walks in his huge pram. He is just starting to talk and, like all babies, points to the scenery we pass, providing the vocabulary I need. Together we explore all the gardens and parks in Kensington.

My life is very free and easy. I am determined to integrate, to not be noticed, to not stand out in a group. Nobody pays much attention to me; here, people seem to mind their own business. This is quite the opposite of life back home. My English improves and, encouraged by Nicky, I talk more. I am beginning to like life in England. Spring has arrived. But I also have to look for work to help with the family budget.

My sisters take me shopping. First stop is Sainsbury's on Shepherd's Bush Green. What a long, cold shop, with its marble counters and walls. I learn that in this country you queue. We buy butter, which the assistant cuts off a huge slab and then shapes with two wooden pats. Similarly the cheese comes in large rounds and is cut off in wedges. Cheddar is new to me. I look for Brie and Camembert and when I ask, I meet with blank looks, and nudges from my sister. Bread and milk are delivered to the top of the stairs outside where we live, six pints and one loaf every day. Mausi takes me to have my hair cut in Notting Hill Gate. The hairdresser says she's never seen hair so out of condition. 'What does she wash her hair with?' Mausi explains that in Germany we did not have shampoo – not yet, anyway. I buy a pair of white shoes with the money I have earned babysitting. They look lovely but they pinch my feet dreadfully. They are my first pair of shoes that have not been handed down, and in my innocence I paid no attention to the leather's lack of pliability – it remained hard and painful no matter how much I wore them.

I learn to go to church and we are accepted grudgingly into the Russian community. They love Papa but see his large family as a burden. Coming from Germany with a non-Russian mother does not endear us to them. The congregation are mainly old women dressed in black. But some are kind and we soon settle into a routine. In my spare time, I read the classics as well as newspapers. After I start work, I pick up the *Daily Express* at the newsagent's outside the Oval Underground station, if I go by Tube. And I read women's magazines: *Woman*, *Woman's Own* and *Picture Post* – anything I can find. My vocabulary improves steadily.

I make the acquaintance of the Labour Exchange, Youth Employment, and I am sent for an interview. I cannot remember the name of the people, but the building is large, on the corner of a bridge across the river. They are looking for an office junior with typing and shorthand abilities. Promises of 'I will learn' are not enough and in due course I receive a 'no thank you' letter.

Mausi, my eldest sister, takes me to an employment agency in Bond Street. They send me to a handbag manufacturer in Islington where they are looking for an office junior. My heart sinks when I realize that not only does the company have a German name but they are also German Jews, who had to leave Germany because of the Nazis, employing English Jews in their workforce.

'They'll never give me a job.' How can they? They'll pour all their hate and anger on to me. Do I need this? Didn't I have enough of name-calling and stone-throwing in Germany? There, in that tiny village school in Michaelsbach, my brother, Victor, and I were held personally responsible for the participation of Russia in the war. I know that as a native German-speaker I am viewed as German by Russians, English and Jews alike. It matters not that I have always been stateless and that the Germans didn't want me either. I go for the interview and am offered the job at £2.10s.0d per week. Suddenly elevated to being a wage-earner, I skip home with my news. Recently, we have moved into an eight-room house, spread over four floors, in Brixton. I can catch the tram at the bottom of our road and rattle all the way to the Angel for the sum of sixpence. I love the journey: down Brixton Road, around Kennington, up to the Elephant & Castle, across Waterloo Bridge, under Kingsway, along Rosebery Avenue (where through the tram window I come across the Sadler's Wells Theatre) in Finsbury and then the Angel. Sometimes I get off the tram at Sadler's Wells on my way to work and I buy a token for sixpence. I stick half the token on one of the stools outside a wall of the theatre. After work, I join the queue, pay another two shillings upon showing my half of the token and from the back of the stalls I see the performance of the day. I get to know a lot of operas and smaller ballets. Sometimes I have to rush down Brixton Road to the Oval and catch the Northern Line straight up to the Angel; when my mother eventually joined us from Germany, she would expect me to do chores before work, which often made me late.

Work is another eye-opener. It is a small firm and everybody is very kind and friendly. Nobody asks where I come from. They all help me with the language. The mother of one of the directors visits about once a week. They speak German, but in a secret sort of way. I keep my head down. The secretary is from English Jewish stock, married to a furrier whose workplace is in Golders Green. She telephones him a lot. Eileen does the accounts and trains me. We like each other. We stay friends until her death and she is godmother to one of my daughters. Her dad is a 'bookie'. I don't understand what that means, except that in the secretary's eyes it is nothing to show off about. I meet the people in the factory. There is Ethel, the supervisor, who comes up to the office in the morning and has a cup of tea with the other director, in the showroom. Ethel wears very high heels, short skirts and always gives me a lovely smile. She is the one I can never understand when I have to answer her on the switchboard. I do not like the switchboard; it's an ugly temperamental box with too many switches and leads.

Within six months of arriving in England I have learnt a lot of my second language, sat an exam, which I passed at grade 2, obtained a job and am finding my way around the largest city in the world.

I become a member of the YWCA, where I meet an assortment of other nationalities, as well as a lot of English girls. Every Friday, they have dances, which I love. I join various groups, one of which organizes walks around the capital; I remember one trip to the

Guildhall in the City. We were taken down to the kitchens. I had never seen so many shiny pots.

In August 1950, Mama and my two remaining sisters arrive in England. World politics have changed. Nansen passports are no longer issued; they have to come to England with German travel documents, which does not please Mama: 'The Germans never wanted me. They had no right to take my Nansen passport when Hitler came to power.' It remained a sore point for the rest of her life, as Britain also did not want her or Papa. They were too old and poor: they both died stateless.

Our family of nine settled into life in England. Papa, always a quiet man, spent a lot of his time in his room, emerging only at mealtimes. He made a point of reading the *Daily Telegraph* every day. His spoken English was poor and his German not much better. He was happiest when talking Russian. Mama was quite the opposite. She learnt English and French at school, adding them to the Dutch she'd learnt when a child. I remember her and her mother conversing in Malay when we were young – Oma would talk and Mama would listen and nod. We would giggle behind our hands at their sing-song conversations and have to be told off.

On very little money, Mama fed her family and the many friends we brought home, as well as furnishing the house. Her greatest joy was the small garden at the back and the minute bit of ground at the front which, in time, was covered with irises. She ensured that as well as integrating into English life we did not forget our childhood traditions. We celebrated Christmas the German way, starting with Advent – lighting candles on the four Sundays preceding Christmas, eating *Plätzchen* (cookies) and singing Christmas carols. The Christmas tree was decorated on Christmas Eve (never before), and after six o'clock real candles were lit and we sang carols, which Mama accompanied on the piano. Presents lay under the tree and were opened after the singing. A festive table came next; I best remember the herring salad with beetroot. On Christmas Day, for breakfast, we had *Stollen* and more *Plätzchen*.

Easter was another feast which we celebrated in the old way: we coloured Easter eggs. We could not get the colours here, so somebody sent them from Germany. And we had *kulitsch* (a traditional yeast cake) and *pascha* (a very rich cream cheese and egg spread) when Russian Easter came. We integrated new English traditions into our childhood ones and considered ourselves fortunate.

I read the small print of my Aliens Certificate of Registration. It tells me what England can offer me. After five years, I can apply for British citizenship. The choice to belong is no choice at all. When I have been here for four years, I receive a letter from the

Home Office confirming that I am now a permanent resident of the UK and can, if I wish, establish my own business. I watch two of my sisters marry and become British through marriage. Nadia goes through the citizenship application procedure, and in 1957 I do the same. I have to find four British-born sponsors, advertise twice (at great expense) my intention to apply for citizenship in the local papers, fill in forms and submit it all to the Home Office. Becoming British will cost £25. I lead such a busy life that I soon forget all about it. The wheels turn slowly.

I leave my very informative and instructive junior office position after four years and get a job with a big electrical firm at the top of Shaftesbury Avenue. One day, my boss receives a call from the personnel department to say that there is a call for me from the police; would he permit me to take it?

Police? Wanting me? What had I done wrong? I relive my whole life in the few seconds it takes me to pick up the receiver. My boss leaves the room immediately. A man speaks to me, identifies himself – in my nervous state I understand nothing – and very quickly reminds me of my application to the Home Office. What a relief!

In connection with my application, he wants to interview me in my home to clear up certain matters. When is that possible? Before I can say anything, he suggests a date which, incidentally, he has already confirmed with my parents, and further informs me that the personnel department has agreed to let me have the afternoon off with no loss of pay! I work in the morning and go home for lunch.

We have spring-cleaned the best room in the house. Mama has prepared a tray with tea and biscuits, which she will bring in during the interview. Who is more nervous, her or me? She warns me to watch out for trick questions. He'll want to know what your real reason is for wanting citizenship. He may suspect that you'll want to emigrate, which would be easier with a British passport. Memories of a German SS officer interrogating us in 1942 float across my mind: he was asking questions because it was known that one of our great-grandmothers had come from the Bordeaux region in France, and he inspected our fingernails closely for signs of Negroid antecedents.

The officer is a young chap, not in police uniform, smartly dressed. He accepts Mama's offer of tea. He wants to know about my friends. Have I any intention of getting married? He's noticed that I am not wearing any rings, but he knows traditions differ in other countries. I say that I have always intended to become British in my own right, adding that nobody will be able to say I'd done it the easy way. He quite understands this, and explains the system and how the application will proceed before leaving.

Some time later, I am informed that I have been

granted British citizenship and I am sent a Certificate of Naturalization. I have to take the Oath of Allegiance within a month to make it effective. I do so on 18 April 1958, before a Commissioner for Oaths. On 29 April 1958, I receive a letter from the Home Office enclosing my Certificate of Naturalization, which has been duly registered. I return my Aliens Certificate of Registration to the police. My Certificate of Naturalization from now on takes the place of my birth certificate and will have to be presented when my death is registered in due course.

Later that year, I marry the man I love, who is as Cockney as they come. We have four children, who are proud to be British. They too have adopted some of my childhood traditions into their lives with their spouses and children. In England, I have always been treated decently and been allowed to think freely. Like my siblings, I have worked hard to integrate, and we have been allowed to belong. I still hate accent-spotters – 'Do I detect a bit of an accent?' – or impertinent questions about my origins from total strangers. It will remain a sore point until my Certificate of Naturalization is presented for the final time. Right from the start, I wanted to belong, to integrate, to not stand out. I quickly dropped my Americanisms and picked up what I thought were typical English expressions, like 'cor' and 'blimey', which after some practice were very effective and confused quite a few people! I came to know and love the church I was baptized into and which we had not been allowed to attend in Nazi Germany.

In 1958, at the age of twenty-four, I finally belonged somewhere and I jumped with joy. I now lived in a country I had learnt to love and appreciate. I was British, I belonged and I was free!

# A Leaky Roof in London

*Nina Joshi*

Sooo many Euro-pyans, I thought. All walking, talking, pushing, pulling, smiling, crying, bags here, children there, policemen in helmets. *They really wear helmets?* I felt a sense of importance, being among all these white foreigners who were going about their business as if it was nothing special. But, *I* always knew I would be a star one day, and here I was.

The night before, at Jomo Kenyatta Airport, I had said a holding-back-the-tears goodbye to my friends, because I was actually quite excited about going. No longer would I jealously read letters from others who had left Nairobi and settled in LA, New Jersey, Toronto, London, with all their talk about snow, famous stars, multi-channel TV and chocolates. Chocolates. I was in the land of proper chocolate, not the type with ants and too much grainy sugar. I was in the land of chocolate and real Euro-pyans. I hadn't come across many of them before.

I had seen Margaret Thatcher on the news – my father had tut-tutted at the screen. And I had watched *Superman* – and vowed to find a special skill for myself, obviously, like flying or saving the world. Other Euro-pyans I had seen, in *real* life, were (a) those who wore very little and swam in the hotel pool near our flat, ordering soda and fat, greasy chips they didn't finish; (b) those who wore a lot and 'took drink' in stout glasses at the Norfolk Hotel; (c) my father's friend who had land in the Kenyan Highlands and a rifle; and (d) a tall boy who joined our primary school for a few months, where the other students were brown, like me, or very brown, like the local locals, who called us Indians *Muindi*.

'Go home, Muindi!' 'Taking our trade, Muindi!' 'Living in our houses, Muindi!' Of course, my friends didn't say that. They said, 'You almost black, Muindi,' perhaps because I didn't attend an all-Indian school. India? I had seen it in films at the Belle-Vue Drive-in, sitting in our Maruti, parked next to crackling speakers on short poles. But I was more excited to see London, with its real queen, double-decker buses, police in helmets. I had a sense that white people – my father called them Euro-pyans – were special.

We all looked up to them, despite knowing they had taken over both our heritage countries of Kenya and India, and they seemed not to notice us. Maybe we all looked the same to them, as they did to us, except for Superman and Margaret Thatcher. But I sensed they, as a people, had a special ability to gain power that we variations of brown didn't. And I thought I, too, could become special, by association. I had learnt that people in foreign countries were *always* special.

'Did you hear she is marrying a boy from York-shaayer? Proper foreign-born,' an aunty would say, with a mixture of envy and awe about the *foreignness*, while slurping dhal and rice and hoarding pink-orange syrupy sweets on her steel plate at a wedding. '*I* was foreign-born,' I said often, but the response was, 'Don't think yourself special,' although never in those words. 'Yes, but you are here and one of us, really.' I was born in London, at Queen Charlotte's Hospital, during a power cut. I suspected *that* made me the opposite of special.

Besides, I knew as well as anyone did, my first steps were off the aeroplane in Nairobi. My first memory is of my neighbour at Popman House stealing my mango. I am told my first solid food was curry and rice. Next was cornmeal *ugali*, and then *uji*, which I preferred because of the sweetness. So landing in London didn't feel like being back home. In fact, it felt like being far from home. And I knew then I was really stock Kenyan Indian, as everyone there had said, not an unusual, exotic foreigner. Still, I thought there was a chance for me. I was going to be living in England. I would even get to visit the house, Aston Villa, that I had read about in class, in my *Objective English* textbook.

It was 3 June 1984 when I arrived in London, with my mother and my Libyan-born and Kenyan-born sisters, to meet my German-born brother. My itinerant parents had secured a house in west London for us. On our first day in the country, we were all wearing scratchy multi-coloured sweaters my mother had knitted, because: 'London is *very* cold. You can freeze in a second.' My younger sister and I whispered to each other that we were hot and sweaty. But neither of us took our sweaters off or talked, until years later, about our disappointment in the flight.

For weeks, as soon as we had found out about the aeroplane ride, we started saving Goody Goody toffee bars, Pussycat chewing gum, lollipops and boiled sweets from other people's houses. We were sure we would get bored for the many days we would be flying to get to the faraway land of the Queen, with its *Cinderella* and *Snow White* palaces and castles. But when we got off the plane at Heathrow Airport, we still had most of the sweets in the plastic jar that Sweetshop Aunty had given us. And it hadn't taken days, only one night. And for most of that we were asleep and didn't even feel faint so high in the sky. It was a total let-down.

The house was dirty and had something called rising damp, which made the wallpaper black and mouldy and the carpets wet and musty. We would all be sleeping in one room, because the rest of the rooms were taken. 'It's temporary,' my mother said. We were to hear that a lot. We cleaned and cleaned and coughed and sneezed for what seemed like hours. When I realized it had indeed been hours, I looked outside, then hurriedly climbed on to the top bunk. 'Look, the sun is still shining,' I shouted, excited, pointing. It was ten at night. A miracle! Surely that went against the very laws of science. If I hadn't seen it with my own eyes, I would not have believed it. But this happened each day for many weeks. Light at night.

In Kenya, six o'clock was the deadline for the sun. Curfews started then, because it was then that darkness fell, in quite a hurry. We had left Kenya with almost everything we owned, also in a bit of a hurry, shortly after a failed military coup. Some of the looting and rifle-firing had been in view of our flat in the centre of Nairobi, located between the police and fire stations. We were caught in the crossfire. One night, when my father was away, our metal-grille fence was pushed and pulled and torn down from its frame. A neighbouring bar-owner, Mutwa, and his gang stopped the attackers, splitting a lip here, cracking a bone there. We didn't go to school after that for many weeks – either it was shut or my parents didn't think it safe. We hardly went out. But in London, also, we hardly went out.

When we did, we heard people shouting 'Paki'. At

first, I wondered whom they were shouting at. When I realized it was us, and that 'Paki' meant Pakistani, I explained we were not Pakistani but Indian by origin, although, I admitted, I had never been to India. They could call us 'Indis' for short, to get our attention. But 'Paki' it was, and I realized it wasn't so much to get our attention. I got punched or kicked for taking the trouble to explain, or spat at, sometimes by one, sometimes by many boys. And I saw neighbourhood schoolgirls putting two fingers up at us.

I didn't know what that meant, but I had heard one of them say 'piss off' once and asked my brother if the fingers meant that. 'It's worse,' he said. I wondered if it meant 'defecate off'. That made sense. Piss was number one, in polite terms. So number two – and they had been holding up two fingers . . . I just hoped they weren't in my school. But no such luck.

To join the local high school, I had to take year-end exams in the ink-paper-wood-smelling hall, so they could check whether I was able enough. I got between 90 and 100 per cent in most subjects, except English history, for which I made up answers – I only knew Kenyan history – and French, for which I made up words. I wasn't surprised by my results. I had covered most of the exam topics two years before, in my primary school. But it didn't make me as popular with the students as I had expected, unlike in Nairobi, where I was looked up to. Only the teachers definitely liked me. Luckily, none of them disciplined with canes, as they used to in Kenya.

There, even *I* had been caned, or told to walk on gravel on my knees, although I was usually best in the year, winning prizes (mostly book tokens) for most subjects, most years. Still I got punished for forgetting to get my record book signed, or losing the inter-schools debate or not knowing the logical but upside-down time in Swahili, which was offset by sunrise. Our home help used to do my Swahili home-work and I still got it wrong, but I didn't want to tell him. Besides, I learnt that smearing lemon juice on my palm before a caning helped lessen the stinging. Sometimes, if I knew the answer, I would have to cane pupils who didn't, which meant I would be in trouble later.

Then there was Mr Stevens, with his straggly, spirally goatie, who often called me into the staffroom and asked me to pick up pieces of bone and meat that he had somehow managed to scatter under the table and chairs. I would do as he asked, because it was usually he who caned me. And as I was on my hands and knees, he would say, 'Indian, eh? Vegetarian, eh? See this Muindi, my servant now.' And he would laugh.

Despite those memories, I missed home, my friends and my school. But I put on a brave face in my letters, making up stories about our life in London – watching

TV, eating chocolates, meeting the Queen and Margaret Thatcher, but not Superman yet. The most joyous time was receiving the replies, except when they talked about problems.

Salome, a girl I used to take food for because she never had any, had asked before whether I could take her with me. I had given her our address, but I knew she wouldn't even have money for stamps; a teacher had taken some skin off her face in a pinching-of-the-cheek incident and Salome had accepted a daily triangular Tetra Pak pint of milk for a week as compensation. In any case, I knew that even if she had a passport it would be Kenyan, and that would be a problem.

My younger sister had a Kenyan passport and my parents had bribed an official to get her out of Nairobi with us – President Moi wasn't happy about allowing Kenyans out. Whenever a guard had walked past the airport waiting room, rifle in hand, we had dived down out of sight and prayed that we would board the plane quickly. My mother then bribed a body-search woman who had seen us duck and threatened to call a guard.

The Kenyan government had also placed restrictions on the amount of shillings that could be sent out of the country, so my father sent £250 a month to us. He had stayed behind to carry on running his college, to earn money and in case things got better.

Only in years to come were we to find out about a machete attack as he locked up the college one night, a mild heart attack and the landlord wanting to oust him and sell the building.

In the meantime, £250 a month didn't go very far between five in London, even though we tried to be prudent, saving coins for the gas and electricity slot meters under the stairs. So my mother looked in the papers for a job. She had been administrator for my father's electronics college *and* taught photography there. She had also been on various social committees. We were sure she would find an office job quickly. But the many places she applied to turned her down. She finally got an evening job stuffing handbags in a small factory. She also babysat for a West Indian family, a Filipino family and an Indian one, who all dropped the babies off at our house.

Although my mum didn't always have time to cook, she showed us how. But we chose to live on baked beans and toast. On weekends, if my mother wasn't working, we would have a cooking project. Samosas. Spring rolls with home-grown sprouts. *Kachoris*. We hated rolling the paper-thin pastry, and soon we too looked for jobs.

My brother repaired electronic toys. My older sister worked in a clothes shop. I delivered leaflets for £1 an hour and my younger sister kept baked beans or spaghetti on toast ready for us until my mother thought she was old enough to come leafleting. I was thirteen, and in the summer holidays I worked every day, from morning till ten at night. It was still light then. I used some of my money for food shopping, when it was my turn, and the rest I put into a bank account I had opened. We all knew what we were saving for.

In Nairobi, we were in a band and had appeared on Voice of Kenya Television, with my older sister as the lead singer. But in London, we didn't even have a working TV. We only heard about the long hours others watched it and sighed each time we thought about the numerous channels we were missing. The TV we had on top of the dresser didn't even flicker with interest when we turned the knob. But my mother was sure my father would be able to repair it when he arrived in several months' time. It was 'temporary'.

And we didn't have a washing machine, but that too was 'temporary'. So my older sister and I washed our clothes in the bathtub every Sunday, sitting with our feet in the lukewarm water, jeans folded up to our shins, scrubbing the clothes with soap and a hard brush. We tried everything to save on electricity and gas so the meters would last longer. It meant we often went to the community centre on Sunday afternoons to heat cans of baked beans in the centre's kettle when no one was looking.

When we *did* cook en masse, it was for good reason. In the summer, especially, we would cook a large batch of potato curry and puris (potatoes and flour were cheap) and carry the huge saucepan between us to the house of one of the families my mother babysat for, alternating between the West Indian and Filipino households because they lived closest.

We would, all five of us, turn up as a 'Sunday lunchtime surprise'. In the beginning, this seemed a truly welcome surprise for them. It saved the mothers cooking. While they got the plates ready, praising my mother for her thoughtfulness, we would play with the children. One of us always had the job of 'accidentally' finding the TV channel showing an Indian movie. As soon as we heard the *dhishoom dhishoom* of the bullets or the *bachaaaooo* screaming of the heroine, we'd all turn to the TV, transfixed.

The afternoon would be spent eating and watching a film our hosts didn't even understand. In fact, often they fell asleep on their sofas while we enjoyed ourselves, cleared up and left. But our hosts cottoned on to our surprise visits and began advising us before the day that they would be out. It was good while it lasted, and we began to think of other potential hosts. I wondered about meeting people in class.

Once school started, I worked every evening, even when it started to get dark at three – another shock – and all day Saturday and Sunday, apart from when my leaflets-boss was away at a party or a wedding, in which case I regretted the money I was losing. I used to think about her, red-haired, smoking, listening to tapes in the smart, black car she used to drop me in faraway streets, in Kensington, Knightsbridge, Mayfair, and nearby streets in Shepherd's Bush, Acton, Hammersmith. I fantasized of one day being like her, waiting in the car while others ran to do my work.

But it was no use. I had to earn money whether she was at a wedding or not. So I took another job, delivering free newspapers locally. I volunteered to post a thousand papers a week, for which I got £10. I soon realized that a thousand houses was a lot. So I gave my younger sister half the money to help me fold the papers, in twos and threes. Then, while she pulled the trolley, with her woollen gloves on, I raced up the paths of the houses and stuffed a few bundles through each letter box. We finished soon enough, but we often got chased all the way down the High Street by gangs, who flashed penknives at us to warn us first, which was thoughtful in a way.

We became better and better at running away. But I heard the word 'rape' one time – the same word I had heard the night of the attack on our house in Nairobi. Although I didn't know what it meant, I sensed it wasn't fun. After that, I told my sister not to come because I was unsure of what to do if something happened. Then I too began avoiding delivering the papers. Instead, I burnt the bundles in the back garden while my mother was at work. I figured the paper wasn't up to much anyway. But I got found out.

Tony, who paid me, had been asking around. When he knocked on our door, he saw the previous week's bundles lying in the corridor. My stories about being sick didn't fool him, and he stopped giving me work, although he was kind about it. I continued with the leaflets, taking care not to ruin that too, looking forward to the weekly highlight: each of us took turns to buy a Mars bar or a Turkish Delight on a Saturday. One of us would use a ruler to measure and cut the chocolate into five equal parts, and we would all savour our pieces while reading our books or comics.

As I delivered leaflets, I daydreamed. And each time I won a painting or writing or crossword competition, I wondered whether that was the beginning of my riches and fame. But the reality was different.

As winter arrived, so did the cold. We had no central heating and never enough leftover money in the budget. So, every evening, we gathered around the oil-filled electric heater, holding our hands out to catch any remaining heat – we had begun to pile wet clothes high on the heater to dry them. When the money in the meter ran out, we rushed straight to bed, all of us wearing several layers under the blankets.

When sleep didn't come easy, I modified in my

head the cartoons that I remembered watching at primary school, in a hot, crowded classroom, before the main Christmas show about Jesus and the Crucifixion, when most of us fell asleep only to be woken up by the purple-attired White Father. Oh yes, he was the other Euro-pyan I had seen. He was soft-spoken, with gold-rimmed glasses, which he adjusted now and again as he put the reels on and took them off the projector, looking quizzically at the film roll when it got chewed up, sweat dripping down his cheeks. Christmas in Nairobi hadn't been cold. The only snow I had seen was at a distance, on the top of Mount Kenya, on the way to Mombasa on holiday.

Excited as we were to see snow for the first time in London – the sheer whiteness of it – we shivered till it hurt. Still, I took photos of us posing and grudgingly spent money to develop them, using a value postal service. We sent the pictures to our friends to show our glamorous life abroad in the snow.

When it didn't snow, it rained and water came through the perforated bedroom ceiling. We moved our sodden beds to where it wasn't wet and brought saucepans and basins to catch the water. We each had to be on rota to wake up and empty the pans every hour. Finally, when most of the bedroom ceiling was leaking, we huddled on mattresses in the living room. There was no money for repairs, and my mother didn't want to worry my father, so this had to carry on until we saved enough or a dry spell came. It was 'temporary'.

Sleeping so close to the ground meant that we heard the mice better, their feet scurrying or sometimes sauntering nonchalantly. The green poison didn't stop them. After my brother found mice droppings in his shoes, we began to empty ours out before wearing them. We fully expected to find a nest of pink baby mice snuggled inside our warm, smelly shoes. When we had visitors, especially from Kenya, we hid this fact from them. 'We don't want pity,' my mother said. I said I didn't mind.

During festival celebrations – Diwali, Navratri, weddings – we wrapped ourselves in sparkly clothes made by my mother or older sister and went by bus, hoping for a lift on the way back. But we lived far from most Indians we knew, who were in north London in warm houses. Still, it was temporary and we mustn't be jealous, we were reminded. So we daydreamed about the house we would have one day, with central heating, a washing machine, a working TV, enough money for electricity and gas, and time to make food. I secretly dreamed of a chef, tall ceilings, a cinema/games room, a driveway, cars, steps leading up to the house, a tiara. I was often jerked out of these moments by a shout of 'Paki'.

At school, many of the students only talked to me to call me 'Paki' or tell me I smelt, which, with hindsight, was a distinct possibility. I hated washing with cold water in the winter, and we were trying to save on gas so I couldn't use hot water. Sometimes a girl would offer a seat next to her, but then would get teased herself. The most popular girl dared the boys to take me out, to which they replied they wouldn't even sit next to me.

A few remarked with surprise, 'At least you speak English, init, and not some bungo-bungo language.'

'Kenya used to be a British colony,' I explained. 'All our classes were in English.' (Except Swahili – not bungo-bungo – and I wasn't very good at it, which was nothing to be proud of at thirteen.) When they asked me if we'd lived in trees, I nodded. 'And we had lions in our back gardens guarding us, killing if necessary.' At least that wasn't completely made up; I had *seen* lions killing gazelles, zebras, antelopes, in the savannah, not quite our back garden. Still, in the grand scheme of things . . .

A few schoolboys teased me about my clothes. I had bought them when I discovered a shop that sold them cheaply. But the boys called me an Oxfam tramp. Finally, to my delight, a group of girls seemed impressed by the brown suede, platform wedge boots I had found in a cupboard under the stairs, where the mice lived.

'Can I borrow your boots for the school disco?' one girl asked.

I was afraid she would keep them. So I said, 'I don't think my mum would like that. And . . . I don't think they are your size.'

The girl and her friends burst out laughing, and one jeered, 'She finks you actually wanna borrow 'em, init?' I had seen similar boots in Indian films. They were very hip in the films, and I wanted to be like the singing-dancing screen goddess Hema Malini, not like these girls who said 'init'.

The bullying continued during my leaflet or news-paper rounds, including shoulder-punching, shin-kicking, rib-poking. My heart raced every time I left my boss's car to walk up blocks of flats or into the High Street, teeming with gangs, even though *most* times nothing happened. I was sure dogs sensed my fear, because they barked madly when I approached doors with 'Beware' signs. Once, as I posted a leaflet, the dog banged into the door, barking, and I fell down the stairs I had just climbed, feeling hot with shame at being so afraid. That evening, a boy walking past flicked my hair and I'd had enough. Obviously, I couldn't tell anyone, because I suspected we all lived in our own purply-green, black and blue worlds. But I decided to make a change.

When my mother came home that night, exhausted from stuffing handbags, I asked and she agreed that I could go back home. She fell asleep before I could tell her how much I had already saved. But her promise gave me a new lease of life. I worked every hour I could. In the meantime, the English as a Second Language class became friendly with me. I had replaced them as the main target for bullying. One of them even protected me from the school bullies. She and I applied for an American penpal, and once again I had moments of excitement waiting at the letter box.

The PE teacher, upon discovering I was from Kenya, asked if I would be their long-distance runner, which I was happy to do, although I had hardly run in Kenya. But I had sprinted many times down the High Street for a mile or so a time, running away from gangs.

A year after we arrived in London, I had enough money for one ticket. The next day, I told all my friends and teachers I was going back home. I promised my new ESL friends I would write. My teachers seemed surprised that my mother hadn't said anything, but I assured them it was an oversight. My friends gave me a farewell card on the last day of term, signed by them and the teachers. I took my money out of the bank on the way home and ran all the way, even though I wasn't being chased. I practised my speech to my sisters and brother telling them I would save enough to fly them back too. I packed my bag and waited for my mother to come home, so we could agree a time to buy my ticket the next day – the start of the summer holidays.

Waiting, waiting, my head lolled and I fell asleep. But as soon as I heard the click of the lock my ear had become attuned to, I woke up, still fully clothed with my shoes on. Smiling, I showed my mother the money. I began babbling about the ticket prices, saving lunch money, plans to help my father.

What I hadn't anticipated was her flat refusal to do 'anything so silly as buy you a ticket to Nairobi'.

I had told everyone I was leaving. I had got a card, signed by even the teachers. How could I go back to school now? My mother looked sympathetic but she didn't change her mind. I discovered years later she thought we had seen enough of people being shot dead, enough of blood in gutters; that she had had enough of worrying every time we went to school or returned slightly late. She told me she too missed her friends. 'I hate this life here. Just *look* at me.' But she had responsibilities. Then, she dropped the bombshell: 'We will never go back there to live.'

I was devastated and returned to school after the summer, to the surprise of my ESL friends but not my teachers. To avoid losing face, I began planning a trip to America to meet my penpal instead. I touted *that* as the reason I wasn't leaving for Kenya. After all, I *had* saved money. There was, of course, no need to tell my mother anything about it.

I didn't make it to America for another few years. Instead, I convinced my family to take a holiday in winter to the Isle of Wight, because, obviously, a beach meant sun 'n' sand, as in Mombasa.

Over time, and to my great relief, I did *finally* make more friends. I even managed to 'share best friends' with another girl. The bullying decreased and I even became protector to my kid sister.

In the sixth form, playing good pool, helping with maths and being agony aunt – living vicariously through classmates who *had* a love life – meant the most popular boy asked me out. And, just like that, I became part of the 'in' crowd. It felt like cheating and I made an extra effort with the remaining outsiders, hoping for a happy ending, convincing myself I was solving the problem from the inside out.

Years later, what I could only have dreamed of happened – being 'Paki' was 'in'. Fate? Hahahaha, buwaaaahahahaha. Suddenly, I could feel proud rather than ashamed, and in oh, so many respects: food, cinema, writing, music. I could make a life in the UK without always looking around for somewhere else. The power of what's 'in', deciding it and bringing it about, became more apparent to me.

Eventually, I fell in love with London and in London, and it became my 'in' city. But recent world events mean that, sometimes, I still need to keep an eye over my shoulder, just in case.

# We are in Heaven

*Toni Jackson*

'We are in Heaven.' This is what my grandparents said when they came to live in Scotland. They had fled, along with many other Lithuanians, at the beginning of the twentieth century, to escape the brutality of the then-conquering Russia. My grandparents were peasants back in their native land and spoke of working in fields of potatoes where mice scurried between their legs, sometimes clinging on to my grandfather's trousers (which were always tied at the bottom with string to prevent the little rodents from getting inside. For my grandmothers, however, it was not so simple, for they wore long trailing skirts which provided the perfect hiding place for the tiny creatures).

My mother's father was, I now realize, a brave and clever man, for it was he who organized the escape across the Baltic Sea to liberty in Scotland. Their days of toiling in the potato fields were coming to an end. Never again would they witness a relative or friend suffering at the hands of the Russian soldiers who rode on horseback, plundering the fields, bayoneting young men and pregnant women. The boat that made the long journey was a cattle ship, and the stench of pig dung and urine was horrendous. My grandparents were told to keep out of sight in case they encountered any enemy boats, so pigs and humans shared the hold.

The crossing was a torturous experience lasting almost two weeks. The only means of sanitation was wooden buckets, which had to be sluiced out in darkness. One young woman, who had hidden her pregnancy for fear of being refused a place on the boat, miscarried and her baby had to be lowered into the depths of the sinister and unwelcoming sea. It was therefore little wonder that my grandparents regarded Scotland as 'Heaven' in comparison to the life they had previously endured.

When the boat docked in Glasgow, they were divided into groups and taken to different parts of the city, where they were housed in tenement flats. (A tenement flat is a large, dark, stone building containing six or eight flats, very typical of Glasgow architecture.) My grandparents then learnt that because of the large numbers of Lithuanian immigrants arriving in Scotland, and because of the long tongue-twisting surnames they had, they now had to take a British surname to make registration less complicated. As a child, I did not give much thought to the matter. As an adult, however, I know that this was wrong. My grandparents, though, were happy and prayed every day in gratitude that Scotland and its people made them welcome.

It wasn't long before church halls were used for Lithuanian clubs, where my grandparents could meet up with their friends for singsongs and dances. They now had their own little community within Scotland and need never feel alienated in a country which my grandparents described as 'too good to be true'. But they found that it was true. They were free to go anywhere they wished and not be persecuted. They could attend a church service and not be afraid that the church would be set alight in front of their eyes. They enjoyed visiting Glasgow's beautiful parks. To sit in peace and safety and listen to a brass band playing in a bandstand was one of the nicest experiences they'd ever had. In one particular park (Rouken Glen), they could not believe their luck when they found a dark damp corner where velvety mushrooms grew. Soon, their babies came along. My mother, father, aunts and uncles were born on Scottish soil, and it was at one of the Lithuanian dance clubs that my parents later met and eventually married.

Growing up with Lithuanian grandparents in Scotland was frustrating for me, for they did not attempt to speak English. Instead they spoke in their native tongue and used only basic English phrases when greeting their neighbours. I listened to a language I never fully grasped, and I regret that I did not pursue it for there are many questions I would have liked to ask them, which remain unanswered.

I do, though, have many wonderful memories of my grandparents. Grandfather used to take me shopping to what would now be regarded as a delicatessen. The shop was run by a Lithuanian man by the name of Adolphus and always smelt strange the moment the door pinged open. Later I learnt that this odour was garlic. I remember the ringed pork sausages hanging from hooks above my head, shaped loaves of brown bread sitting in huge wicker baskets and enormous jars of gherkins pickled with herbs and peppercorns sitting on wooden shelves. When Grandfather had paid for his goods, Adolphus would then (and only then) open a jar of sweets and allow me to choose two.

The nicest memory, or perhaps the most amusing memory, I have of Grandmother is of staying with her and Grandfather during the school summer holidays. Across the road from where they lived was a baker's shop and on a Friday afternoon, as a special treat, Grandmother would take me to choose some special delight for our supper. On this particular occasion, there was a large queue stretching from the counter outside on to the road. Inside, in perfect rows, was an assortment of cakes and buns. Eiffel Towers all coconutty and pink, Paris buns with their lumps of crunchy sugar and studded with raisins, cream horns dusted with icing sugar and plump strawberry tarts oozing crimson jam. I just loved to gaze at this beautiful display as the queue moved slowly forwards.

At last it was our turn to be served and Grand-mother raised her hand, displayed three fingers and said only two words: 'Cherry cake.' The lady behind the counter reached over to pick out three fairy cakes, each of which had a bright-red cherry on top, when Grandmother got angry and said, 'No, no, cherry cake, cherry cake.' By now, everyone waiting behind us in the queue was taking notice and saying, 'Cherry cake?'

The assistant serving Grandmother was by this time quite flustered and moved towards slices of cake which had cherries and icing on them, thinking these were what Grandmother wanted. But no. Grand-mother was so frustrated that she tapped angrily on the glass counter directly above the strawberry tarts, saying, 'Cherry cake, cherry cake,' until the assistant realized what she meant and picked up the tarts. The assistant, Grandmother and everyone in the shop, including myself, breathed a sigh of relief and Grand-mother and I went home with strawberry tarts for supper.

I also remember my grandmother receiving a letter from her sister, who was left behind all those years ago. The letter came in a flimsy yellow envelope (almost the texture of an old newspaper which has been read and reread many times). When the envel-ope was opened, I (even as a little girl) felt a sense of foreboding when I saw that certain words and sentences had been crudely cut out of the paper. My mother explained that the letters between Grandmother and her sister were often censored to ensure that no description of either country, good or bad, was exchanged. As the years slipped by, the letters from Lithuania ceased and we did not know if it was because Grandmother's sister had died or if a stop had been put to the correspondence.

I am now a grandmother and always remind my grandchildren of their great-great-grandparents and of the long, hazardous journey they made, almost a century ago, across the sea to Scotland. When my grandparents were asked, shortly before they died, if they would ever like to return to Lithuania, they said the very same words as when they first arrived in Scotland: 'Why would we want to go back when we have everything here? We are in Heaven.'

They were eventually laid to rest in a cemetery in Glasgow. On their headstones, my parents had their names inscribed in Lithuanian. We were certain that this is what they would have wanted, for in death nothing is complicated.

# Goodbye, King Wenceslas

*Mimi Chan-Choong*

It was rare to have 'a foreign little girl' at an English school just after the end of the Second World War. Everyone thought I looked and sounded German. Maminka made me wear my blonde hair in two long plaits, tied together in a top-knot on the crown of my head. In the looped curl of hair, she threaded a fresh daisy or any other flower she could find in the garden.

She brushed out the tangles every morning. 'You have to suffer if you want to be beautiful,' she chanted firmly.

I wanted a hairstyle like the other girls I had seen walk past our house: a short bob with a full fringe. After I left the house with my older brothers to go and play, I shook my head violently to make the flower fall from my hair. If it didn't, I yanked it out and threw it into the grounds of the nearby cemetery.

I was almost five years old when I began at St Mary's Roman Catholic Infant School in Uxbridge. Up until then, I had spoken only Czech or German, Czech with my family and German with our home help, Anna. Anna was sixteen when she came from Germany to our home in southern Bohemia. Her mother had died and her father wanted her to set to work. Anna came with us the night we escaped Czechoslovakia and fled to England.

On my first day at St Mary's, the headmistress, Miss Hoey, told Maminka that I had to learn English before I could join the regular class for my age. I was allowed to attend the art, music and gym classes, but I had to stay behind after assembly to take language classes. I watched the line of children trailing out from the hall to their classrooms.

Miss Hoey beckoned to me across the hall and I joined her on the podium, where my lessons began. She was wearing a white blouse with a deep-purple skirt and matching cardigan. There was a bow-shaped brooch pinned to her chest with trailing ends covered in sparkling stones. Her hair was short and silvery. It bounced and shimmered when she moved her head.

We started with the 'Hail Mary'. I chanted the final line over and over again: 'Nava java debt arrrmen, nava java debt arrrmen,' until it echoed the other children's words. 'Now and at the hour of our death. Amen.'

Miss Hoey was a patient teacher and praised my handwriting as I wrote lists of new words and phrases into my tall, grey vocabulary book. I enjoyed memorizing nursery rhymes about 'rings of roses', poetry about 'wandering lonely as a cloud' and prayers addressing the same God we had in Czechoslovakia.

I learnt the phrase: 'Well done, dear, that is very good indeed.' She stroked my hair and smiled down at me, immersing me in a cloud of her perfume, 'Midnight in Paris'.

One morning, Miss Hoey told me that it was time to join the other children. After the morning break, she took me by the hand and we walked to Miss Lee's classroom on the other side of the playground. It was a long wooden hut resting on rows of short brick pillars, with a black metal chimneypot on the roof. I was sad to be leaving Miss Hoey's lessons but excited to be joining the new friends I had made in the playground. Holding the cold, wet metal handrail, we climbed up the three steps. Miss Hoey knocked on the door and opened it immediately, without waiting for a response. Inside, I saw a tall, cylindrical stove on a stone plinth, with red embers glowing in its small glass window.

The faces of forty children turned in my direction. They were sitting in pairs at double desks in straight rows. Miss Hoey announced to the class that I was going to show them all how much English I spoke. I gripped her hand tightly and she did not let go.

I started quietly, half-singing and half-speaking 'God Save the Queen'. Miss Hoey started to clap and everyone joined in. Then I began 'Land of Hope and Glory'. After the first two lines, Miss Hoey started to sing too. By the end of the song, everyone in the room was belting out the lyrics. The same happened with 'Rule, Britannia' and I started to relax. Miss Hoey let go of my hand as I began chanting the 'Hail Mary'. After I uttered the last line, 'Now and at the hour of our death. Amen,' Miss Lee directed me to an empty seat and I put my collection of vocabulary books inside my desk. By the time I looked up, Miss Hoey had left the classroom and I watched her silver hair bobbing out of view through one of the windows.

'Arms folded and no fidgeting,' barked Miss Lee. The girl in the next seat nudged me and showed me how to fold my arms across my chest. I copied her and she smiled at me.

Even after I joined Miss Lee's class, I continued weekly English classes with Miss Hoey. My desk filled up with the tall, grey vocabulary books.

As I walked around Uxbridge town with Maminka, I always carried my dog-eared vocabulary book with me. I wrote down the words I read on signposts: 'Municipal Pool', 'Police Station', 'Keep off the Grass' and 'Magistrates' Court'. I kept the wrapping papers from sweets: Sherbet Dips, Black Jacks and liquorice sticks. While we waited in queues, I scribbled down 'ration books' and 'coupons'. I added 'cod liver oil' and 'malt' before Maminka poured spoonfuls down my throat.

Like many post-war children, I was underweight for my age and was prescribed 'sun lamp' treatments, which went straight down in my book, as well as 'Guinness'. Our general practitioner, Dr Mandler, suggested an iron-rich diet and explained that the strong black drink was an excellent source. Maminka gave me a glass of the bitter-tasting stout every evening before bed.

Dr Mandler was Czech and his surgery was a few stops away along the railway line at Ruislip. Maminka preferred to take us there for our check-ups because she couldn't understand our fast-talking local doctor, who was from Scotland.

My brothers and I played in the derelict buildings of Uxbridge. There was an abandoned railway station called Vine Street, which was a favourite haunt for local children. We climbed the abandoned wagons parked in the sidings, trying to push them along the rusty rails without success. We sometimes met up with other children and spoke a mix of languages together, including Gaelic, Welsh, Yiddish, Polish and Italian. Language was no obstacle to our games.

At school fêtes, Tatichek played his violin and sang Czech folk songs, while I danced around him, waving red scarves in the air. He had a honeyed voice and all the parents crowded around to listen. I wore national costume, which Maminka had hand-sewn for me, twirling out my full skirt with its layers of white petticoats and my apron embroidered with meadow flowers. In my hair, there were matching daisies, cornflowers and poppies – white, blue and red, the colours of the Czech flag.

After our performance, I took my father's charcoal-grey hat around the crowd and collected money for Miss Hoey's school fund. As I shook the change in the hat, one man asked me where I was from.

'*Czeskoslovensko,*' I replied, smiling.

'Oh yes, that's Yugoslavia,' his wife said.

'Isn't that one of those communist places?' he asked.

There was always lots of confusion about where we were from. At the greengrocer's stall in Uxbridge High Street, Split Plum Bailey thought I was Hungarian. He taught me the names of all his fruits and vegetables and helped me to write the names in my vocabulary book.

'Sank you wery muchk,' I said politely, as he handed me a squashed pear, oozing juice out of its cracks.

He laughed when I failed to pronounce 'th' and 'w' correctly, and I laughed with him, happy to be able to take the fruit home. He gave our family dark wooden boxes stamped with 'Fyffes' on the side, as well as pine crates that held Seville oranges. Tatichek turned the boxes into our furniture and toys and I copied down the exotic names, like 'Jamaica', 'Spain' and 'Tunisia', into my vocabulary book.

The local shopkeepers' children became our friends. The Novaks ran the tailor's, the Polaks had the bakery and the Mallachs, whose father was a

German ex-prisoner of war, ran a flower stall in the local market. There were the five Clerkin boys, the Sayers and dozens of Finnigan kids, who were a wild sort but I liked them a lot.

We picked cobs of corn from local farmers' fields and hid behind bushes, popping young peas into our mouths. We pulled up potatoes and cooked them in the ashes of our bonfires, crunching their crisp, cindered skins.

We found 'treasures', colourful electric wire and old porcelain spark plugs, on the town dump, which we kept in secret boxes. We made drinking cups from discarded envelopes and toasted each other, calling out 'slangivar', 'yaki dar', 'na zdravi', 'prost' and 'bottoms up', before gulping down our favourite drink, Tizer, 'the appetizer'. I filled up the pages of more vocabulary books with my new words.

My parents were also learning English, using the phrasebook *English in 500 Words*. Their grasp of the language came slowly and while they tried to learn to live in England, Maminka recreated a Czech home for us in Middlesex. Our house was decorated with pictures of Prague Castle's spires, shrouded in mist, St Vitus Cathedral with plum trees in blossom and Charles Bridge, with its statues watching over the River Vltava. In my bedroom, a painting of King Wenceslas, which I prayed to every evening, looked down at me. Our curtains were made from hessian sacking cloth, on which Maminka hand-embroidered poppies with long green stems. She painted her own pictures of the snow-covered hills around our village, Velhartice; of the church of Saints Cyril and Methodius, where her brother was the priest; of a little girl in national costume, with long blonde plaits, crying into a bunch of flowers.

The first person to speak to my mother was Cissy Hudson, a chubby Irish lady with cascading chestnut hair, who pushed a huge forest-green pram with 'royale' inscribed down the side in gold. I wrote the word 'royale' in my vocabulary book, and Miss Hoey explained it was to do with a very important person who lived in a palace. She crossed off the last letter with red ink.

Cissy Hudson's pram was filled with freckled, red-headed children bouncing up and down in the well-sprung carriage. She did not wear a hat or gloves like the other ladies who walked past our house. They never stopped by, but Cissy Hudson came in regularly for coffee and cakes with us. She taught me to sing 'It's a Long Way to Tipperary' and 'Danny Boy'. Every Tuesday evening, she picked up Maminka and they went to the Mothers' Union, where Maminka made new friends among the Irish community.

Tatichek maintained strong links with his former army colleagues, and our families met up at weekends at Velehrad, the social and religious centre for the

Czech refugee community in London. The men wore their wartime medals to the Sunday services and the children dressed in national costume. After church, my brothers and I joined the other children to study the Czech language and national history under Father Jan Lang, who, in spite of being a Jesuit priest, was an expert at singing beer-drinking songs. He helped us to prepare Easter and Christmas celebrations, including concerts for our parents, followed by big buffet dinners and dancing. These were noisy gatherings, with accordions pumping and loud singing, leaving crates of empty Pilsner Urquell bottles. All the women helped prepare the food, laying out platters of rye-bread sandwiches, salami, gherkins and pickled fish. There were cakes and pastries dusted in icing sugar and piled high like snowy hills.

During the week, Tatichek worked at the local builders' merchant, and at five o'clock, he would return to clean their offices for extra money. If I was home, he would take me with him on the back of his bicycle. He moved from room to room, sweeping the floors, while I scooped up the small piles of dust and litter. In the typing pool, there were typewriters under black, leatherette covers. I learnt to spell words like Remington, Olympia and Olivetti while Tatichek swept. Afterwards, we lifted down the chairs from each desk and I sat down at a typewriter and pretended to be a secretary. Gently lifting the cover, I pressed the keys to watch them jerk up and down. I took a sheet of paper from the wastepaper bin, carefully entering it under the roller, and typed out lists of everything I could see in the room. I couldn't type Czech words as there were no squiggly accents.

On Fridays, Tatichek received a brown envelope containing his wages, £5.2s.6d. I was often sent to pick up supplies from the Sherwin Sisters' shop in the High Street, writing down Camay Soap, Sunlight Soap and Kiwi Shoe Polish as I walked around the aisles.

In time, Tatichek had his own shop close to Paddington Station. It expanded from selling fruit and vegetables into a continental delicatessen, which he named London Street Stores. All the staff were refugees and we opened from eight in the morning until eight at night, with half-days on Sundays.

I did not see Tatichek so often now but we ate much better than we ever had. Rationing had ended and our larder was filled with food from the shop: fresh poppy-seed rolls, Black Forest ham, fat frankfurters that popped with juice. There were ropes of onions, peppers and garlic hanging from the ceiling, and cold meats from Hungary, Yugoslavia and Italy were laid out on the white marble meat shelf. There were rye breads and pastries from the Polish and Austrian bakers, dark pumpernickel from Germany, sweet Jewish cholla, Irish soda breads and Scottish oatcakes.

London Street Stores became a hub for the immigrant community. They came to the shop to keep in touch with their lost homes, by eating the foods they were familiar with. The provisions came mainly from Robinski's Wholesalers, who had big storehouses behind Wormwood Scrubs Prison. The two Robinski brothers wore white hats and white coats like doctors, lifting their hats and bowing slightly whenever Maminka and I went together to place an order.

During the holidays, I loved helping at the Stores. I talked to the Irish nurses from St Mary's Hospital, the West Indian porters from Paddington Station and the 'painted ladies' from Sussex Gardens, who wore white-rimmed sunglasses and very high heels. We learnt how to greet our customers in Sinhalese, Arabic and Swahili. We put the takings in a red Oxo tin, which we hid overnight inside a hessian vegetable sack.

As the shop grew larger, my parents worked harder and I was sent away to boarding school. Maminka said she wanted me to become a proper lady so that I would be able to fit in in England. But St Bernard's Convent School in Langley was actually run by a French order of Cistercians and the students were from all over the world. My friends were Teresa Tibuligua from Uganda, Catherine Mariano from Sudan, Huan Tran from Vietnam, Beatrix Viney from

Venezuela and the tiny Unglass sisters from the Solomon Islands.

Maminka was right though. The Cistercian sisters tried to mould us to fit into society. All the 'foreign girls' had elocution lessons from Miss McGovern, who, we were told, spoke the very Queen's English. We wore straw boater hats and white gloves with our uniforms and learnt to curtsy to the senior nuns when we passed them in the corridor.

I became close to the sisters who worked in the kitchen and the laundry room, who were mostly Irish. They hitched up their robes when they worked, tucking them into their thick leather belts, revealing their white petticoats, and tied their black veils in a knot at the nape of their necks.

Sister Patrick and I sang the Irish folk songs Cissy Hudson had taught me, and she turned a blind eye when I scrumped gooseberries, apples and plums.

'You'll get collywobbles eating unripe fruit,' she teased playfully.

One morning, she caught her hand in the laundry wringer, crushing three fingers. I watched in horror.

'*Boze muy je to hrozny*,' I cried out. ('My God, this is terrible.') I still slipped into Czech in times of anguish.

'Don't you fret,' said Sister Patrick reassuringly. 'I shall name them God the Father, God the Son and God the Holy Spirit.'

I prayed every evening, pleading for the Trinity to

make the fingers grow back. I ran my fingers over my rosary beads, which had been blessed by the Bishop of Northampton. When praying did not work, I questioned the Mother Superior.

'Reverend Mother, didn't you say "ask and ye shall receive"?'

'You have asked for the wrong things,' she replied coldly.

I found the school rules hard but I enjoyed my classes. With Czech, German and English under my belt, I was strong at languages and added Latin and French to my repertoire. I had vocabulary books for all my languages now. I loved French with Sister Alphonse, who was very elegant and supposed to have been a Spanish countess.

History classes were an endless list of kings, queens and battles. When I asked Mother Hedwige if we could study Good King Wenceslas of Czechoslovakia, she told the class he was not a real person.

At the beginning of every term, Maminka and I took the 457 bus from Uxbridge down the Bath Road to Langley. The fare was ninepence for both of us. She carried my big suitcase and I carried the canvas holdall. Two years after I started there, Tatichek picked me up in our new car. It was a very shiny Black Humber Hawk with white-walled tyres.

I loved washing that car and scrubbing the smudges off the white tyres with a Brillo pad. I polished the walnut dashboard until I could see my reflection looking back at me. Eventually, I learnt to drive it along the gravel lane at the back of our house that led to the woods, where I had made my first friends.

A good few years later, one of the customers at London Street Stores came in to collect her order. I was attending to the till while Maminka unloaded a tray of Royal Sovereign strawberries. The stylish lady approached me.

'I was served by that foreign woman last week,' she said, pointing to Maminka. 'Here is my receipt.'

'Ah, you mean my mother,' I replied quietly.

The woman was taken aback. 'Oh, how funny, you don't sound foreign.'

I looked up at her. 'But I am,' I replied.

# Where is Home?

*Cliff Walker*

I was born on Antigua, in the Leeward Islands, in the part of the world then known as the West Indies but today generally referred to as the Caribbean. There was war in Europe, which would later be the cause of my journey away from my island home. My passage into this world was, by all accounts, not exactly easy or pleasant for my mother. It was rather a difficult birth, although it should not have been. It was a home delivery, on the first floor above our small grocery shop. Father, conveniently, was on his rounds, a point not missed by the midwife or my aunt, my mother's sister, who was assisting her.

My father was due back any time The funeral cortège of a well-known 'fancy man' (my aunt would say 'Rogue') was passing by. As the hearse approached, so did I and my father too. 'As one goes, another arrives,' said my aunt, who had a deep dislike for my father. She never, even to her dying day, admitted to whom she was referring – to Father or to me – but she always used to say to me whenever I did anything to displease her, 'You are just like your father.'

I was born encased in a sack. The midwife, and I
am told she was qualified, cut a small hole in the bag
so I could breathe, gave my bottom a smack to get
my lungs working, as they did in those days, and went
to watch the funeral procession go by. It was thought
to be a lucky omen for a baby to be born in such a
sack. He or she could expect to gain fame and fortune.
Normally, the child is quickly removed from the bag,
which is then preserved and treasured. But in my
case, by the time the midwife returned, the bag had
stuck to my skin and had to be peeled off in bits and
pieces, taking some skin with it. This, I was told later,
was not lucky. So there went fame and/or fortune.

And so it was that my life began. A life that was to
take me from the shores of that small island to many
other places, initially to England. But why did I and
many like me make the journey in the first place?

My mother told me that at the end of the 1940s
Britain began actively recruiting in the West Indies.
British Railways, London Transport and the recently
formed National Health Service sent teams out to
encourage people to come and help in the rebuilding
of the UK after the war. And come they did – my
mother and sister and all. And so it was that I
journeyed to join them. My father wanted nothing to
do with it. The war had been enough for him. He
stayed in the West Indies but he did not stop me going.

Four thousand plus miles in a boat on my own – a

mere boy, not yet fifteen. I had only been away from my island once before and that was to a sunny place. I had never experienced winter. I had never felt the cold or seen snow. I did not know what it was like not to have feeling in my fingers or toes, what it was like to have my teeth chatter without direction from my brain. I was soon to learn about these and many more unpleasant things, not all associated with the climate.

My journey started in a small boat, which took us to the ship lying at anchor in the deeper waters outside St John's Harbour. Antigua was its last port of call before the voyage across the ocean began. On board were others from other islands, all going to seek a better life in England. There were about 120 people in our party. Seventy or so young unaccompanied men, ten married men travelling with their wives, twenty-five unaccompanied young women and five of us children, between twelve and sixteen years old, all going to join their parents. None of us had ever travelled such a distance before. All the children were supposed to be supervised by an adult for the whole of the journey. My supervisor was to be a young woman of about twenty-two years of age. I was introduced to her as I got on board but that was the last I saw of her. I guess she had other things to do, other interests to pursue.

The ship was not what you could call comfortable.

It had been either a troop carrier during the war or a banana boat, or maybe it had been both. We were separated into men and women – even those who were married had to part. Four or five to a cabin. My cabin had two bunk beds, which was about all that you could fit in. Two of us standing side by side filled the space between the beds. Another person would have been more than a tight squeeze. I was given one of the top bunks, which I had to climb on to using the frame, as there was no ladder or steps. The cabin, I am sure, was one that would normally have housed the on-watch engine-room staff. It was right next to the engine room. You could hardly hear yourself speak without shouting and sleep was impossible. The crossing lasted fourteen days.

At the end of it, the ship docked in the Italian port of Genoa, a quaint little town with cobbled streets. The war had now been over for ten years, but the place still showed signs of the ravages of the conflict. From there it was the Boat Train to a port in France, across the English Channel to Folkestone, and finally Victoria Station in London. It was a grey November morning in the mid 1950s. I had reached my destination, almost. Would Mother be there to meet me? It was snowing. I stood on the platform, a young boy all alone among strangers in a strange place. For the first time in my life, I was afraid. A crowd of people, many black, were there to meet their families and friends, arriving as I was from the West Indies. Would Mother be among them, I asked myself again.

I stood on the platform, looking into every black face – searching for the one that would take away my loneliness. I was with hundreds of other migrants (most of whom were much older than me) but I felt very much alone. It was cold, very cold. I had never known anything like it before. My face was burning. My ears and my nose were sore. I had no feeling in my fingers. I could hardly hold the small suitcase in which I carried my earthly belongings. The shoes I was wearing were not suitable for the time of year, neither was my clothing. I had no overcoat. The longer I waited for that face to appear, the more desperate and cold I became. I was almost on the point of tears. I wished I had never left my home – my island in the sun.

'My son, my son, Cliff, Cliff, are you here?' came a voice I knew. But where it came from I could not see. There were what seemed like hundreds of people coming and going. It would be hard finding her. She was, after all, only about 5ft 4in tall – the crowd towered over her. 'Mother, Mother,' I cried, 'where are you?' Suddenly, she was there. I looked at the woman beside me, the one person I needed more than anyone else right at that moment. It was good to see her again, to be with her, to hold her, to tell her that I loved her and to feel safe in her arms. 'Oh,

Mother,' I said. She held my hand, saying, 'You are freezing. Here, put this coat on and these gloves.' The last part of the journey was by bus, to the part of London that would be my home for the next few years.

Life in London was, oh, so different from what I was accustomed to at home. In Antigua, we lived in a house in the town and had a fairly large house in the country, surrounded by its own grounds and near to the sea. The sun shone every day and there was never any need for a fire to warm the house or to heat the water to have a bath. Life was fun. I wandered wherever I wanted to. Swam in the sea, played games with the other boys and did not have to be indoors before it got dark. I was no different from most other children, in colour or in the way I spoke. Neither was ever an issue for me. Life was good.

But in London, things were all different. There were fires to warm the house, a house that was always cold. And everything seemed to matter: your colour, your accent, your very existence seemed to cause problems for others which were not always easy to resolve.

The house was divided into flats. Mother's flat was on the ground floor. The next two floors were occupied by other migrant families, a family from the West Indies on the first floor and an Irish family on the second. (It was common in those days to see vacancy notices which read, 'No Irish, No Blacks, No Dogs.' So migrants shared what accommodation they could find.) The flat consisted of two bedrooms, a kitchen/diner and a bathroom/toilet which we shared with the first floor. The kitchen/diner led to a small yard, with an outside loo, where the dustbin and my old bike were stored.

Not that I got much opportunity to ride the bike. Because when I was not in college classes or at the dental workshop where I was an apprentice, I had to be in the house. I was locked up, so to speak. A prisoner, no longer free to roam wherever I wanted. I had no friends. I was alone.

Mother was concerned that as the only black boy in the area I was going to get myself into trouble, fighting with the local lads who were usually hanging about outside the house. I found that she was right when I ventured out without her knowing. I had to fight to survive.

What had Mother done to me? Bringing me all this way to have to fight for my life almost every day. I wished I had not left my home. But fight I did, and suddenly I am in. The other guys accept me. I am, in a way, one of them: a fighter. They turn their attention to another boy who has recently arrived. He is different from them, but not in the same way as me. He is Scottish, a 'Jock' they say. He will have to be given a bashing. I know what will happen to him, if he is not a fighter. I may have to look after him. We become friends. Two boys in a strange land, different but with a lot in common.

A year passed; more black boys arrived. They were older than me, young men really, but we became friends. And, of course, there were girls, and the bluebeat house parties every Saturday. But girls could be trouble. The white lads did not take too kindly to having 'their' girls going out with black boys, and often neither did the girls' families and friends. Black girls were in short supply and knew it. They were, as the saying was in those days, 'facety'.

On Saturday mornings, I was required to be on hand to assist the dental nurse prepare the patients from the old people's home to see the dentist. Many of those old boys chewed tobacco and some had not used a toothbrush for years. And having to work on a Saturday morning, when every one of my friends was off work, did not appeal. It was not very long before I quit. Life was there to be enjoyed, even if there were difficulties to overcome.

Another year passed, and Teddy Boys and others were roaming the streets, looking for trouble. There were fights between blacks and whites, for no reason other than the colour of their skin. Any black lad on his own could find himself in danger. We travelled in numbers for safety whenever we went out. One boy (Kelso Cochrane) was caught on his own in Notting

Hill, on his way home from work. He was killed. No one was ever caught. 'What have you done, bringing me here to get killed?' unfairly I asked my mother.

What I had to do was to get away from London, away from the fighting and killing. Get away to the country to the kind of quiet life that I had enjoyed only two or three years before. Getting called up to do National Service was very much on the mind of every male over the age of eighteen. Indeed, some of my friends had received their papers and were already joining the Army. I knew what I had to do – I had to join one of the three armed services: the Navy – I did not relish all the swimming I might have to do. And all the marching if I joined the Army. The Royal Air Force it had to be then. But how was I going to join without getting Mother's approval? I was not yet eighteen years of age.

I had that bridge to cross, but first there were the entrance test and medical to pass. I was summoned to the Recruiting Office in Holborn and duly passed both tests. Soon I had to convince Mother that joining the forces was what I wanted. Eventually she was persuaded by the idea that she could 'buy me out' at any time in the first twelve weeks, if I didn't like it. I also had to sort out the little matter of the girls – Sylvia, Barbara and Josephine. Josephine lived some distance away, but the other two were close at hand. 'Who should it be tonight?' I said out loud. Mother and my sister both laughed. 'One moment you are worried about dying – and it may yet be the case if they find out about each other,' Mother was saying. 'I am your baby, you would not let anything happen to me. You will protect me, you love me, you said so yourself,' was my reply.

The girls did find out, with a little help from my sister, I think, although I can never be sure. And so it was time for me to go. To see what the rest of the country, and the world, had to offer, via the Royal Air Force. Life in the RAF was not what I expected. People shouted at me, asking if there were any more like me at home, calling me all kinds of names, none pleasant, and doubting whether my mother even knew my father. The only thing they seemed to have no questions about was my colour.

They made me stand for ages on a parade ground, holding a rifle, or march up and down. They taught me how to fight, how to shoot, how to kill other people. What was this all about? Was this not what I was running from when I left London? This was not how it should be. I had got it all wrong and this time I could not blame Mother. She had not wanted me to join up, she had wanted me to continue with my studies and become a dentist. She feared that if I joined the forces I could get hurt or even killed in some far-off land. She was almost proved right. I did not get myself killed, but in at least one of the overseas areas where I went to serve people shot at me. People I did not even know, who didn't know me. I had to get back to the safety of England. I was now married with a wife and children, and they were my chief concern.

But in England, other problems returned. I was sent to Gloucester but had trouble finding accommodation for my family. I would make an appointment to see a house only to find that it was no longer available when I arrived. The same place, however, was very much available when a white friend made enquiries a short time after.

The signs were no longer up but if you were black, there was no room. It was hard to find somewhere to live and when we did, it was usually rented from a fellow migrant and by the gods you had to pay, and you were expected to obey whatever house rules were set: no visitors after 8 p.m., no overhead lights after 10 p.m., no this or that. Not even the drill sergeant was as demanding as some of those landlords, who knew they had the upper hand and played it to their advantage.

My time in the RAF was not without incident; getting promotion, being told that, because of my race, I could not work at certain tasks I was trained for or get an embassy job, were issues I and others like me faced. But generally, time passed and then it was time to return to civilian life. After nearly twenty-five years, I decided to hand in my uniform. I was once again a civilian, looking for a quiet life in the country.

Before leaving the RAF, and while serving in Germany, I had bought a house in a little Cambridgeshire village. And so it was that on my retirement from the RAF I at last found my quiet place in the country.

I am now a Cambridgeshire man and a deputy to the Lord Lieutenant, an honour that, among other things, allows me to say 'thank you' to my mother for bringing me all that way and for meeting me on my arrival. I feel sure she would be proud of her son today. I know how she must have felt back then, meeting me at the station. My daughter was away in the USA for two years. I remember how I felt on her return, meeting her at the airport. She had come home.

So where is home? Home for me is where my children and their children are, and that is here in Cambridgeshire. But I do still yearn for my island in the sun, which will also always be home to me.

# The Gentleman of Reigate

*Ali Sheikholeslami*

Very true. Just as I had expected. One look is sufficient. Merely seeing that emblem and the odd letters on the crimson jacket of the passport is enough to wipe any trace of a smile off the face of the potentially gentle man on the other side of the thin line. The line that I must cross to be able to officially claim I am in the UK. The same line I need to cross to continue my studies.

'Government of the Islamic Republic of Iran . . . PASSPORT.' That's what I have. That's what I give to the immigration officer. Apparently, the passport alone is not enough. What counts is the yellow, pinkish piece of paper on page eighteen, with a tragically sad photograph of me on the far left of it, a silver crown neatly touching the top of my hair. 'No recourse to public funds' – well, whatever. The passport man makes sure to thoroughly read the UK Entry Clearance glued to this page at least eleven times. He looks just like one of the nerds I remember from school, who were not remotely interested in the contents of the books, but they kept reading and studying and memorizing and getting the best marks and being rewarded for the best performance. In a deliberate offensive, he asks me things I cannot digest. A polite, obviously tense 'pardon me' makes him repeat the attack, this time more fiercely and slightly louder.

Why am I here? For heaven's sake, it says in the 'type' section that it is a student visa. Why would I be here with a student visa? To peel potatoes? Hunt hippos? Of course, I don't share any of these thoughts. I explain that I have a student visa, and the reason for that is because I have been accepted on a postgraduate course, and I show him the formal acceptance letter and my translated degree certificate and my transcript. And my bloody bladder is bursting and this guy keeps asking me irrelevant questions that take ages. He gives a final look at every single line of each page, moving his head to the right, to the right, and to the left, to the left.

He gives the impression that he has discovered the biggest ever possible criminal, an Al-Qaeda-related alien from the 'axis of evil', a Corleone-related mob head, or perhaps Hitler's long-lost aide. I'm on the verge of bursting. I mean into tears. I feel utterly defeated and totally expect to be deported any second.

The big man stands up. His rise resembles Goliath's against David, a mighty move. He grows and I feel even smaller. He comes to the other side of the line, to my side. He orders me to follow him. That's it, I'm done. He's taking me to Inter-bloody-pol, or MI007 or some place like that. Following him for twenty-odd yards seems like the journey to Kandahar.

We stop just outside a room with lots of papers and clips, odd posters on the walls, a tall mirror and an exhausted NHS nurse. The passport man stops and spins around, and the corners of his dark lips move up by 2.6 mm. I can't hide my excitement. Now with a much mellower tone, he explains to me that I have to take some medical tests before entering the UK. He is even kind enough to explain that it is not just me, that anyone coming to stay in this country for more than six months has to go through the National Health checks.

The exhausted nurse, who's had a tough day and I'm sure is unhappy with her pay, is upset about her colleague getting a promotion and is still angry with her husband, who never remembers what they had for supper the night before, is apparently not that interested in checking my chest. She just forces a smile and a signature on my papers, and politely implies it'd be better for me if I buggered off.

With all my papers, my hand baggage, my full bladder and my mixed feelings, I squeeze to the other side of the line. 'Sir, sir!' someone shouts, ominously. I halt with my heart beating a million times a minute. I take a deep breath and gather the courage to turn back. They're talking to somebody else.

*

It's out of this world to have a friend waiting for you when you arrive from another country, with the prospect of staying rather a long time. It's even nicer if your friend is a native. It is brilliant if he is a driver and is picking up all your excess baggage, all the funny books and kilos of pistachio nuts and almonds. It is awesome if this friend of yours is wise enough to know about the page-18 'Police registration within 7 days of arrival' thing, and he advises you to do it right away on the way home.

You're at Gatwick, so Reigate sounds a good idea. Off you go. You get to the Reigate Division of Surrey Police and it looks dead calm, so calm that it takes the officer five minutes to come out of his comfy den after our annoying bell-ringing ritual. He happens to be extremely gentlemanly, civil and kind. Your friend pats you on the shoulder and tells the policeman, 'We're here to register an alien.' The policeman frowns and looks at your friend with dramatically raised eyebrows and answers, as if he's wholly heartbroken, 'We no longer call them aliens. We now have a register of foreign nationals.' And he's off again to fetch his register. The gentleman of Reigate comes back with a notebook the size of six or so ordinary notebooks, puts it on the desk, hands you some papers, and then suddenly you and your friend and the policeman see prominently printed on the cover of this notebook: 'The Register of Aliens'. And you all laugh, and all the tension dissolves.

But you know that it's going to be the same every time you take a break, every time you are behind that line again. You know that you shouldn't expect to be welcomed by warm smiles. You know the fear of aliens is something that won't go away in a day or two.

# No Way Back Where

*Marek Kazmierski*

There's something incredible about being an exile. In our wide-open world, when intercontinental travel and multicultural dialogue are no longer the privilege of the wealthy and the adventurous few, being an 'out-' as opposed to an 'in-sider' can be a thing of incredible value. Of course, for most of those forced to flee their homes by persecution, discrimination or mere economic necessity, the reality of exile is far from romantic. But speaking for myself alone, having arrived in the UK from communist Poland as a child of political refugees in 1985, I look at those both born and settled in the same land all their lives and pity them.

Like all forms of pity, it is an ignorant, small-minded thing, but that's how I feel. I'm proud to be a compound soul. Not a product of one source, one culture. The stuff I am made of is alloy, stronger than any single substance, and I can't imagine what my life would be like had I and my immediate family not made our escape those twenty-odd years ago. And although the experience of exile is always painful, even when your new home is a kingdom of relative security and tolerance, mine is a tale I take pleasure in reliving, because it is full of wild colour and amazing fortune – all down to the fact that I have been afforded two countries to call 'home'.

Yet, while talking about my past is an opportunity to express many things, to explore complex feelings, it also allows me to explain why, having spent most of my life in the UK, I am leaving. Why, although I understand full well that there is no such thing as 'going back' for anyone, not in time or in space, I am still slowly but surely making my way back East.

Poland, 1973. Trapped between western Europe and the Soviet empire, not yet recovered from several centuries of invasions, partitions, pogroms and occupations, my motherland was a difficult place to be born into. Sick of conflict and external influence, some Poles struggled from within, often risking the welfare of themselves and many others, to question the relationship with our mighty 'red friend' from the East. Others escaped abroad, to the West and beyond, seeking a different, less troubled life.

My parents were caught in the very eye of this schism. Following a youthful spell as a communist, my mother became a member of the anti-regime Solidarity movement, an ambitious collective of disgruntled workers and dissident thinkers. She was of

the latter breed, a young, well-bred university lec-
turer, happy to drink and talk her way through endless
meetings and late-night parties, where she always
managed to shout the last word. My father, in absolute
contrast, a simple steelworker from a farming brood
of ten, grabbed his first opportunity to leave for
London, on 12 November 1981. His luck was in –
just hours after his departure, a high-ranking general
declared a state of martial law, sending tanks into the
streets, shutting both borders and lines of outside
communication for years to come.

By the time he managed to take off, for what
seemed like 'good', I was eight years old and already
painfully aware of the political realities which framed
every aspect of our lives. The 1980s were a time of
severe rationing and even harsher oppression. My
home town, Warsaw, a place that 'saw' enough 'war'
in a single century to give anywhere second thoughts
about its future, was still, in effect, rebuilding. The
Germans, with Soviet compliance, had destroyed
some 90 per cent of its architecture, before retreating
to surrender and begin the restoration of their own
homeland (with vast sums of US money, handed over
in an effort to stabilize the former Third Reich). Yet
Warszawa (to call her by her native, more evocative
name), in spite of Soviet attempts to keep it reduced
to rubble, was not just rebuilt – she was reborn. Rising

out of her own ashes, she became a symbol of national pride, of hope restored, in spite of the murder of around a fifth of Poland's people.

Considering such harsh facts now, I feel privileged to have been born into a city with the heart of the phoenix. In spite of the shortages and restrictions, my childhood was a time of immense vividness and excitement. I hardly ever remember being at home after school; I was free to play outside in streets without traffic and parks without closing times. Always allowed to stay out until dark, I grew up with no fear of drug dealers or paedophiles or any other fake bogeymen. Communism did not provide prosperity for all, rather poverty for both the intelligentsia and the proletariat, and yet even that was in some ways communal – without 24-hour television/work/shopping, families were tightly knit, the relationship between city and countryside just as close, the taste and colour and texture of everything innately organic. Except for the chosen Party few, everyone had it hard and everyone suffered, and yet the suffering was bearable, because everyone knew communism wasn't everywhere and certainly not for ever.

My father's exile obviously cast a shadow on the closing years of my childhood, yet I clearly recall the sweet side effects to his being 'out West'. Although there was no way of knowing if we were ever going to see him again, from time to time he would send us a package of western goodies or a cassette on to which he had recorded his voice and a few British and American songs (precious sounds in a state where all phone lines were tapped and even the airwaves censored). The odd pair of blue jeans, or shoes with Velcro fastenings or soft toilet paper became humble yet also impossibly glamorous promises from another reality. I remember sometimes crying into my pillow at night, missing him, but our extended family and circle of friends were so large that there was rarely time to feel sorry for yourself. And, of course, there was always the ever-present hope that one day, rather than have him return to our impoverished home, we would join him in exile.

Eventually, and very suddenly, in 1985, long before perestroika would thaw, at an unforeseen rate, the low-level terror that was the Cold War, my mother, my younger sister and I received our long-awaited passports. At the time, it was a document most Poles had no chance of ever seeing, but, after three years of judicious application of both bribe and blackmail, our escape towards reunion was about to be made good.

I struggle today to recall what that moment of rupture felt like. Not allowed to say or write how we felt about most things, we didn't, I suspect, allow ourselves to feel much at all. As difficult as it was to

leave family and friends without a word of goodbye
(for fear of being overheard by someone, anyone,
with corrupt connections), without knowing if we
would ever be allowed to return (staying abroad
beyond the term of one's visa meant severe penalties
upon return), the parting seemed easy enough. The
West, Britain, London, all sang to us with such a
powerful promise of freedom and possibility, we felt
we were going to a much better place.

That our arrival quickly turned into a nightmare had
nothing at all to do with the welcome we received
from London, or its natives.

We landed just after my twelfth birthday, the week-
end the first Live Aid concert was aired in 1985.
Although we had arrived from a land where fear,
hunger and violence were a daily reality, our suffering
had been nothing compared to that of the starving
millions projected on to giant stadium screens all over
the Western world. This was also the year Elton John
released a song called 'Nikita', with a video of him
cruising round Berlin in an open-topped, chauffeur-
driven Rolls-Royce Corniche, pining for a soldier-girl
manning Checkpoint Charlie.

Today, it's difficult to put into words what I feel
about such pop-political statements. Instead, I'd rather
recall the initial amazement of walking London's fast-
moving, multi-ethnic streets, discovering shops with

fully stocked shelves, colourful clothes and advertisements and a sense of relative calm everywhere. The first time I walked into a local newsagent's, its Asian shopkeeper, the first brown face I had ever encountered, handed over a free Twix chocolate bar for me and my sister to share. That shiny gold wrapper, the joy of finding two bars of chocolate inside, the sense of the exotic and generous were amazing.

This, sadly, was one of the few pleasant moments of our new life abroad. Unable to attend school with our non-existent English, we spent the next six months sitting in a grotty flat above a high-street launderette, listening to our parents tearing three and a half years' worth of strips off each other. It was a pattern they would hold, without break, for the next decade. Neither my sister nor I had had any idea that my father's departure back in 1981 was not just a working holiday but also an attempt at a marriage-saving separation. The attempt, alas, was a tragic failure. As long as my parents had been 'at home', with the support and supervision of families and friends, their relationship had kept from imploding. Exile, far from patching up their differences, simply magnified their mutual incompatibility and turned each moment of contact between them into all-out domestic war.

In spite of our 'reunion', my father had no intention of surrendering the mistresses he'd acquired in our absence, and my mother (who, as she would often boast, had enjoyed her fair share of lovers throughout their marriage) shut herself away from the world, ashamed of no longer being considered blue-blooded, drinking herself into a state of absence which has lasted, also without a break, for the past two decades.

Meanwhile, cut off from our support networks, my sister and I got on with learning English by watching daytime TV soaps, with titles like *Falcon's Crest* and *Sons and Daughters*. To this day, I have an accent that is somewhere between London, Dallas and Sydney, a unique mix no listener has ever been able to decode.

Eventually, I was sent to a 'language unit' in Southall, a kind of prep school for the children of refugee families, readying them for assimilation into mainstream education. I was one of only two white kids in this austere, severely under-funded establishment. Morning assemblies were a stunning sea of singularly brown faces and glossy black hair (Nearby Hounslow back then had London's largest population of migrants from the Indian subcontinent). The only other students were a rather mean and unhappy Polish girl, whose name I can't recall, and Nereyda, a beautiful, mixed-race girl from Colombia. She must have been the first dark-skinned person I ever befriended but I don't remember that ever being an issue between us. She was tall and kind and her radiant smile was a rare blessing in a difficult time. Although neither of us spoke any 'proper' English, I remember us laughing together every day, two speechless yet somehow communing exiled teens.

Then, after barely a month considered ready for proper schooling, I was transferred to a local secondary. Nereyda and our silent understanding were replaced by a thousand boys in black uniforms (in Poland, no one wore suits and ties to school, and the idea that genders might be separated during their most formative years was unheard of ). It was a painful transition – an English tutor back at the language unit had taught us to expect corporal punishment and the wearing of shorts and little caps throughout the year. Violence I did not fear so much, but, coming from a country where winters regularly saw temperatures drop below minus twenty degrees Celsius, I was terrified of freezing to death on my first day of real school.

Of course, the said 'tutor' must've been a warped character, an 'exiled' reject from the world of official education, dumped in a place where he was free to scare refugee children out of their wits. The school I was sent to had a wonderfully mixed-race population, high standards of teaching and no canes in sight (outlawed in all British schools some years back). On my first day, my form tutor told me I had a lovely accent and sat me down with a group of boys who would remain my friends until our final exams, some even until today. And, of course, we wore woolly blazers, long trousers and warm hats when the weather turned cold, although the odd icy spell which passes for winter in London is no match for the white wonder years of my childhood.

When, afforded the status of 'political refugees', we were allotted a council flat on the poorer south-east side of London, I convinced my parents not to transfer me to another school closer to our new home. Instead, I cycled every day back to the west of the capital, all through winter, to the same school I had only just started at, so as not to have an inferior education (or be forced, once again, to adapt to a whole new environment). On top of my thirty-mile daily bike ride and finishing my homework, I was out doing any odd jobs I could find. At fifteen, I was working in an off-licence in Peckham High Street, watching British, Caribbean and African customers drinking the same discount booze and insulting each other with equally racist put-downs. Having seen my father cheated in every deal he ever made with his fellow Polish immigrants, I learnt quickly that it was not where you came from but how you carried yourself that matters. By the ripe age of sixteen, while studying for my GCSE exams, I was working as a part-time staff manager in a large high-street shop, earning enough to pay for all my clothes, my music, even a motorcycle. All this allowed me a new escape, away from domestic war and into a future I could construct on ever more independent terms.

After finishing secondary school, I went on to take my A-levels through an exchange programme at an all-girls' convent school near Richmond-upon-Thames. Ashamed of my impoverished background and unsure of my own potential, I watched from afar as floppy-haired boys from local public schools got all the attention. Had I known then that having east-European cheekbones and a motorbike and a troubled past would have got me endless sympathy from the pretty, middle-class waifs, I would have been happier with myself. Much happier. Soon after I enrolled, I fell in love with a charismatic siren from leafy, middle-class Chiswick, a dark-haired, blue-eyed drama student who broke my heart with such force that I spent the next couple of years hiding from the lunch-time crowds, painting and writing as if possessed, crying myself to sleep far more often than I had when my father was exiled from us, only a few years before.

Following this new experience of rejection and loss, I committed the next decade to becoming a writer of powerful stories. Literary success seemed connected with inner development, though I never considered international travel as a way of expanding my horizons. I finished university, but, unlike most of my peers, I stayed in England, volunteering in hospitals, running a restaurant, working in offices, in security, in both the penthouses and the basements of my adopted homeland. I met a number of wonderful women, some born British, others passing through, without ever finding the one who would help stop me in my tracks and settle for good.

I certainly felt no longing to return to Poland, feared it rather, worried that the precious Neverland of my childhood would have vanished after encountering its post-Soviet realities. With no support or security in my daily life, facing the indefinite future of a struggling writer, I feared losing the one place I could still call home – the memory of my motherland. Eventually, though, exactly ten years on from our escape, and a mere five since the end of communist rule, I braved a month-long trip around Warszawa, then the Baltic seaside in the north and the Carpathian highlands down south, all framed by recollections from my earliest days.

Poland turned out to be an amazing place to visit – my vast family happy to see me, my hard-earned pounds sterling affording a rare taste of financial freedom, the whole country running high on a renewed sense of possibility. I made the 30-hour coach trip back there around a dozen times in the next five years. Then, in 2000, struggling to finish my first novel in a humble Brighton bedsit, I decided to move 'back' in a more permanent sense.

The plan was to live in Warszawa for a year, teach English, finish the book and return to London to pursue publication. I wanted to write in a different environment, and part of the story was set in Poland anyway, but I also wanted to stop being a 'tourist' and see what it would feel like to live there again, full-time.

I ended up staying for almost two years. A decade since the collapse of communism, everyday existence was still far from easy – bureaucracy continued to rule people's lives, shopkeepers were as rude as in the days of state-owned commerce and the place had a slightly worn and dejected air about it. But I breathed differently in Warszawa. I walked its streets discovering new friends, old childhood haunts, nooks and crannies that spoke to me in a voice I had not heard in London or Brighton or Peacehaven. The scene of so many recent historical struggles, it was a place where it was easier to question, discuss and understand one's place in the world there. In the daytime, its heart would beat with the vigour of somewhere only just emerging from a long, bitter winter. At night, by contrast, the capital was so still that even the traffic-light system would be turned off until morning. Everyone I met had a story to tell: the young of their hunger to learn and tackle the future, the not-so-young of their complex and dramatic past. I wandered Warszawa's broken pavements and ancient parks, listening to the myriad voices whispering out of every courtyard and slowly opening door, and never felt lost, never alone.

Moving 'back' again to London, the finished novel at the bottom of my suitcase, I found the transition harder than when I had been a speechless, powerless child. I started to earn a decent wage, teaching English to refugees in the community, kept writing and got published here and there, but it did not matter where I walked or who I met, I continued to feel alone. What little family I had left in London, the few friends from my school or university, did not make up for the absence of the spirit I had discovered on the other side of our continent. I tried to relearn how to enjoy the large-scale buzz of my other capital, but every time I drove or flew back for a quick visit to Warszawa, I could not shake off the feeling that my life was upside down – I was living in a place I should've been passing through, and passing through a place I should've been calling home.

People often ask if I feel more Polish or British, and I've always answered with the stock phrase: 'I have a Polish heart and a British head, and that is why I am happy.' Most people smile and ask me to explain. The chemistry behind the statement is simple: Poles are passionate, romantic creatures but all too chaotic in their thinking. Because of its geographical location, caught between the ever-warring strongholds of Europe and Asia, Poles have always had to be good at fighting, even when there was no one around, save ourselves, to battle against. Brits, by comparison, are their opposites – not having experienced a single invasion or territorial conflict in a thousand years, they have the grace of a nation used to a peaceful status quo. Being who I am, born in Poland, matured in England, I believe myself to be the best of both worlds.

I've always thought of Poland as my metaphorical mother – the one who raised me as a child, letting me play in innocence, while also strengthening me for the challenges ahead. Britain, in turn, seems to have become my father figure – responsible for my becoming a man, a hard yet necessary discipline.

But now, in my thirties, a fully grown and independent adult, I find such simplistic sentiments cloud rather than clarify my perception of self and the world around me.

The more I think about my own experience of migration, the more I realize we are all exiles. Every stage of our lives involves some kind of expulsion – first from the womb, then from the innocence of childhood, from the irresponsibility of youth and eventually from the ego-centredness of pre-parenting age. All the time, we are forced to move on in directions we do not choose, and this is why the experience of real exile can help us define who, and where, we really are.

These days, my actual father rarely returns to see his numerous siblings, and my long-lost mother only experiences Poland from the confines of her council flat, looking back through a mad haze of imported satellite TV channels and drink-fuelled rage. And while my sister is settled in London, with a husband from war-torn Angola and their beautiful, cappuccino-skinned daughter, I feel something calling, pulling me elsewhere.

Recently, I have found it ever more difficult to pronounce many words in either of my native tongues. When I am speaking English, my Polish roots are showing, and when I am speaking Polish, I'm all too often lost for words. While this worried me at first, I now realize it is indicative of a sense of development – of no longer needing to sound perfectly integrated. Not that long ago, I was being paid to rid my students' English pronunciation of accent. Today, having travelled the width and breadth of a newly borderless Europe, running various migrant support and art projects I have founded in the UK, I tell everyone I work with to take pride in their individual identities and accentuate all that which makes them unique, language included.

Also, for the first time ever, I find myself truly free

to choose where I want to call 'home'. Finally free of parental or governmental or financial constraints, I can live and work wherever I like. I hold both Polish and British passports, yet the choice of where to go next is not straightforward at all. The more I consider the idea, the harder it is to think of myself as a 'national'. Polish? English? British? None of these labels fit, because they are not specific enough. What do I have in common with the wild highlanders of southern Poland, or the troubled peoples of Northern Ireland? My experience, it seems, is more sharply defined. Defined not by nations but by two cities which have helped raise and shape who I am today.

And today, I am forced to own up to a painful truth: I no longer want to live in London. It is an amazing place, a haven for so many, yet although I feel a 'part of' it, I don't think I, or anyone, can ever be 'at one' with a metropolis. I know this is a severe state-ment, but in speaking from the heart, I need to do so plainly. Thinking of London, I cannot help but feel tired. It is such a single-minded creation, there is no way for it to stop changing, to ever sleep, for it is always in pursuit of tomorrow. Britain's capital was founded by migrants, thousands of years ago, arriving and making camp where the River Thames was still wide enough for large boats to navigate. Its founders did not choose London. London, all by itself, chose us. Sail further towards the source of the Thames, on to Richmond, Windsor, Oxford, and there you begin to discover Britain. But those of us emerging from this most amazing of capitals, a state within a state, must ask ourselves how valid the crest on our passports really is.

Me, I am one-part Londoner, two-parts 'Warszawianin', even though almost two-thirds of my life has been spent in Britain. Since my return to the UK five years ago, I have helped others with pasts that mirror mine, working with migrants and refugees in prisons, in the community, defending their rights, recording and publishing their stories, teaching them the law and the language of their new home. Yet although I want to continue this work in different parts of Europe, including Britain, I cannot stay here.

London does not need me half as much as I once needed it. I know it will not miss me once I leave and will find someone to take my place the moment my few belongings get shipped East. Part of my story is set here, and my immediate family remain, but Warszawa, by comparison, is calling loud and clear. Today, as so often in her past, she needs her children back from exile, with new skills and new visions to help make up for lost time and continue the process of reconstruction. Having survived so much, so many wars, both domestic and external, she is, at the end of the day, more me.

# My Painful Journey

*Jade Amoli-Jackson*

No one leaves her home unless she is running away from something or someone has driven her away. I am telling you, I have first-hand experience of that.

We were born in northern Uganda – my twin sister, Jane, and me. We studied up to Makerere University, where I met my husband, the father of my three children. Our father was a teacher, and later became a reverend of the Anglican Church of Uganda, in Lira district. Our mother was from a well-off family. Her granddad had many herds of cattle, other livestock and farms. So it was no surprise when her dad became the first person in her district, Apac, to own a car. Our father made a good living for himself and became a rich person too. He bought a bicycle when he first started out, and then a car and a tractor. We were brought up with plenty to eat and had a very good education. In class we always came first, or second – and we weren't very happy if that happened. When I was eight, I fought my cousin, who was a chief's son: I was number one in my class in the end-of-year examination and he was third, but he went around telling people that I copied his work. So I fought him, and I won. My sister Jane did engineering at university and I studied media. Afterwards, I worked in television and radio as a sports reporter and got married to my husband, who was a captain in the army, and we began our life together.

We had a farm and we had plenty of food, herds of cattle and other livestock. I had a shop, which was doing very well. Part of it was a bar, where people came and drank in the evening or watched football, if their teams were playing. We would really have a good time, especially during the World Cup, when most of us would support England. I would put a big England banner on the roof and if you supported another team, you were not invited to join us. In my country, I was a rich woman and my three children were doing very well in school. Until, in 1985, the government changed.

One day, when my husband had just returned from the farm and we were eating lunch, five government soldiers came to our house and said the big man wanted to see my husband. At first I thought they were taking him to a barracks in our town, but when I went and checked I found out that he had been taken to Kampala, 300 miles away. I went to Kampala the next day to find out what had happened, but no one could tell me where he was. After two weeks, I went back again with the equivalent of £300 to bribe the soldiers who were holding him, only to be told he had been killed. I had to bribe them to release his body to me. He had been beheaded and I buried him without his head. It was the worst time for me and my children; seeing their father without a head, it really affected them.

We went on with our lives as well as we could for a few months, and then my father and my sister, Jane, were killed by a gunman for ten head of cattle. I blame myself, because my sister wanted me to go with her to Kenya for the day and I told her to wait, because I was consumed with grief for my late husband. That was the day she was killed. I mourned my sister and my father for a long time. My children gave me strength but they were not to be with me: they were abducted on 13 January 2001. To date I have had no news, though the Red Cross is looking for them. For four months, I went everywhere, searching like a zombie, and then I too was abducted, with several other people, some of whom were shot dead. After two months of captivity, hardship, rape, hunger and burying my friends, a soldier helped me to escape from my kidnappers. I was a walking skeleton with wounds all over my body, most of which are permanent. I arrived home, where my little sister and other people gathered when they heard that I – or at least my skeletal body – had returned. My little sister gave birth then but passed away as soon as the baby was born. All these people did not want me to know about it, but I heard their whispers and promptly took an overdose of Valium. But they heard that too and made me vomit it all out.

It is good to be very nice to people, even if they are not related to you; that's why I am still alive. Before our troubles began my husband and I helped a lot of people, financially and physically, to cross over to Kenya when their lives were in danger. The boy who helped me escape was returning a favour, because I had taken his parents to Kenya and paid all their expenses. They were wanted by the government because they belonged to a political party that did not support the government's policies. Another man helped because I had taken his sister's family to Nairobi. But even though I had lost everything, I didn't leave my country voluntarily. I had three beautiful children there, and five nieces, and many orphans, widows and widowers to look after; how could I leave them behind? Even when everything was taken away from me, my children, my home, my livestock and my dignity, I didn't intend to go. I was very ill, unconscious, when I was put on the plane. When I woke up, I found myself in Britain.

I arrived in London, at Heathrow Airport, on 29 July 2001. I was told where I was after three days; the rest was oblivion. I woke up to see this white man looking at me with kind eyes, and the first thing I asked was where my children were, and could he, please, let me see them. I think he said yes, but then I went back to sleep. When I woke up again, he was with his girl-friend, Juliet, and the worst thing was she was black. Though I am black too, I felt so scared that if I could have walked, I would have run out of that room like a flash before she could hurt me. I think she guessed what I was thinking because she spoke to me so nicely. I was on a big bed with a large white cover which, I later learnt, was called a duvet. I did not have that in Africa: we use sheets and blankets because it is very warm out there. The room was painted with flower designs and very cosy, but the lights were blinding me so I covered my head and went back to sleep, which I did a lot during those days.

Juliet was very patient with me, very kind and really beautiful. After a week, I started accepting food, which I did not like at all; even the tea was very different from the tea I used to drink in Africa. She noticed that I did not like the food, so one day she cooked sweet potatoes, spinach, even green bananas, which came from Africa. She also bought Ugandan tea bags. I thought, how could she have gone so quickly to Uganda and bought these foods and tea? If you had told me then that I would come to love British foods I would have said NO, but now I like British foods, even tea.

I started to trust Juliet, letting her near me and

allowing her to touch me, and she helped me clean the wounds all over my body. She and her boy-friend, Andrew, travel a lot to Africa, and that's where they had met the two gentlemen who helped me, who became their great friends and brought me to them in London. Juliet told me that she is also from northern Uganda. When her parents were killed, the neighbours sold their cars and bought air tickets for her and her sister and brother, and they got out of Uganda before the soldiers found them. She was just fifteen, her sister twelve and her brother six when they left. She and her sister and brother helped me a lot with whatever I needed. I was so grateful for their presence.

When I was a bit better, they told me they would take me to the Home Office in Croydon because it is illegal to live here without reporting to the authorities. They drove me to Luna House and I went in alone. I had to leave them outside. I was so scared because they were the only people I knew in London, my only family. It was the most difficult time for me, since it brought back all the nightmares I went through in Africa. I didn't see Andrew and Juliet again that day or for four days afterwards. I thought it was all my fault and that I must be a very bad person. That is why everybody I love is taken away from me.

Luna House was a very big, crowded and noisy

place; there were hundreds of people of all colours and ages. Mothers and fathers with children, young girls and boys, older people like me. But why was I the only one with wounds all over my body and why were my children not with me like the others'? I cried my heart out, not aloud, but with uncontrollable tears coming out of my eyes. I missed my children, my home, everything!

I waited for a long time and then a lady asked me if I had hay fever, because of the tears. She interviewed me, and then I was sent to another section and then another before I was ushered out through the basement into the back of a van. There were two others in the van, a lady who told me she was from Kenya and her five-year-old daughter. Funnily enough, I had stopped crying, but the other lady was crying now and saying she had never been in jail. I told her that there would be no problem since the people taking us were white. The driver had told us that they were taking us to Oakington and that the drive would take about two hours. My legs, bum and all my body were seriously hurting and I had a splitting headache. I had not eaten anything since that morning, but I was not at all hungry. I was just in pain. Sitting on the seat at the back of the security van was hard enough, but with wounds all over your bum, your thighs and all, would you feel comfy? My right leg and arm, all the right side of my body were and are still stiff. I wanted to kneel down, but I couldn't on my stiff right knee. They had said it would take only two hours to get there, but it took ages.

On arrival, we were led to a big room. After some time, they called me into an office, wrote down my details and took a photo of me. A funny thing happened when they told me to look into the camera. I just opened my mouth wide and put my tongue out as far as it would go. I really didn't know why I did that. Maybe I was losing it!

Around midnight, we were taken to our rooms. We were eight in a room, and each of us had a bed and bedding. We were also each given a towel and face cloth. Since I had nothing except a blouse, a skirt, a bra, a pair of knickers and a pair of sandals, and most of the girls I was sharing the room with had suitcases, good clothes and many shoes, I felt sheepish. But then I was taken to the office and given a nightdress, and a very nice lady told me that they would give me more things in the morning.

I could not sleep because I was in terrible pain. I kept turning and crying all through the night, and the lady next to me noticed and told me to tell the ladies working in the office the next day. In the morning, most of us had a shower and we went to the dining room, which was very big. A man in uniform held me gently; I was not afraid of him because he was white and would not hurt me. There was plenty of food, but I could not eat. I tried to make sure no one noticed, but they did, because a man in uniform told me to eat a little and that he would take me to see the doctor. I say a man in uniform because I did not know that we were in a barracks until some months later, after I got out and read a form with the heading 'Oakington Barracks'. I was shocked, because we had really been treated very well. We were given phone-cards to call our friends and relatives, but I gave mine away because I had no one to call. I didn't even know Andrew and Juliet's phone numbers.

After breakfast, I was taken to the interview room and asked if I had a lawyer. I said I didn't, so an English lady called Edel said she would be my lawyer. I told her that I had no money to give her, but she said she was going to represent me free because I deserved to be represented; and since she was very nice, I believed her. She told me not to sign anything unless she was there with me. On the second day, I was interviewed by a lady from the Home Office. I told her, in Edel's presence, my whole story, and she felt really very bad and asked if I wanted coffee. Edel was surprised – no one had ever been offered tea or coffee before. Edel told me that the lady was very important in the Home Office. She shed tears while I was telling my story and she asked Edel to take me to the doctor so that they could examine me and treat me.

The doctor asked me very many questions, which made me cry because I had to relive my sad story all over again, but she was also very nice. After examining me, she gave me tablets for the pains and three sleeping tablets; she told me to leave two of them in the office. I think she thought I would take all of them to try to kill myself, as I had before, and I would have, because I still wanted to end it all. Edel asked her if she could book me in to see a doctor at the Medical Foundation, which helps the victims of torture. I did not understand what they were talking about at all, because I was not a victim here. I was a very bad person who deserved the beatings, multiple rapes, starvation and all the bad things I got. I thought I was the one who had made all those people die or be captured and taken to the bush. If I were a good person, my children would not have been taken. My husband, my sisters and my father were killed because of me, so why should they call me a victim of torture? I told Edel not to let the doctor waste her time booking me an appointment at the Medical Foundation because I am very bad.

They went ahead and made the appointment for 11 a.m. on 18 August 2001. I think Edel also asked those people to let me go since I was so ill, because I was told I was to go the next day. I did not want to leave because the people working there were really very kind and friendly to all of us. There were men playing football and volleyball, children running here and there, young girls making themselves beautiful, and you could see them getting very close to boys or men in the compound. I stayed in the sitting room, lying on the sofa, because of the pain and the guilt of what happened to me, and because of my children not being there like those other children with their parents. I felt I was the odd one out, so my best friend was the sofa. Though the TV set was there, I did not watch it unless other people were in the room. I felt very dirty. However many times I bathed, I was still dirty (and I sometimes bathed as many as ten times a day).

On the third day, at around 2 p.m., the coach took me and other people to the railway station for the journey back to London. I was given a transparent plastic bag to carry the things they gave me, which to me was very normal. I travelled with the men from Oakington to King's Cross and took a bus to Juliet and Andrew's, and they were very happy to see me back. The following day, Juliet took me to see her GP, where my blood was taken to test it for HIV and other diseases. The GP, Dr Cochran, also gave me a lot of tablets for my high blood pressure and other ailments. I really wanted to test positive for HIV so that the people who raped me would die of Aids, but I didn't want the children who were also raped to die of Aids from me so it really tore me apart. When I went back for the result, the nurse told me I tested negative and she said I should be glad. But I was not happy at all, because those rapists were not going to die soon, they were going to rape other women, children and even men. I felt I had let down all those people who I was with in the bush. I wanted to avenge my friend with a three-month-old daughter who hanged herself and her baby after they were both raped. We were forced to bury them in a very shallow grave. I have nightmares about them to date.

So I sat by the road and cried when I left the surgery, and a man who told me his name was Billy came and sat near me and kindly asked me what was wrong. I told him how I had let my friends down because I had thought that I would kill the rapists but I tested negative. He was very patient, and told me that I had shamed the rapists and that my other friends still in the bush might not die, but if I had tested positive, they would, even if they escaped. He said I should pray for my friends who were dead now and for those still held captive, so that they could escape like me and live. He walked me home and explained to Juliet what had happened and asked her to keep an eye on me. I think that if he had not walked by at that moment I might have done something drastic to myself. I could think of a million ways to end it all, like running in front of a car or a bus or any fast-moving object which could kill me.

On 18 August, I went to the Medical Foundation in Kentish Town. At the reception, I told them my name and a very nice lady took me to the waiting room, which was warm and lively with lots of people waiting for their turn to see someone. I had come to see Dr Susan at 11 a.m. but had come an hour early because I didn't know how to find the place. The lady told me to take a seat and she gave me a cup of tea and biscuits. At first I would not take it, because I had no money, but she told me that it was not for sale and that everybody was free to take as many cups as they wanted. After drinking the tea and eating a biscuit, I felt better because I was really hungry since I had not eaten dinner or breakfast. At 11, another lady came and called my name, and when I answered she told me she was Dr Susan. She was tall, beautiful and very kind, and I am telling you, I knew I was in very good hands. She told me that her office was on the first floor and asked me if I could manage the stairs, and I told her I could although it would be difficult. I limped beside her and it took some time to get to her office. She walked as slowly as me and never complained.

She examined me and saw that I was covered in wounds, but she never made me feel dirty, as I knew I was. She asked me about everything that had happened to me and my children, and she said she would book me an appointment with the Red Cross. She also booked me in to see Dr Selza, a psychiatrist, Mary, a therapist, and Liz, a physiotherapist at the Medical Foundation. I saw Mary in the Foundation garden, full of flowers, trees and fruits. There was a pond, which at first reminded me of the swamp that used to be home to me and my fellow captives. I feared going near it, especially when the ducks made it dirty. But I loved the garden, which also had a healing area on one side. Mary and I planted some of the plants from the nurseries, and I went to see them every two weeks.

I joined the garden group, which at first I did not like at all because I wanted Mary for me alone and thought other people would take her away from me, but we became one big family and I forgot my jealousy. Mary really helped me by introducing me to people. I met Alem, who is our support worker at the Refugee Housing Association and took me to the Refugee Council Learning and Integration Unit, where I met Andrew and Vesna. Andrew taught me to use a computer. He also showed me how to apply for a work placement, and I have been doing volunteer work at the Refugee Council every day now for almost two years. I did not know that there were people who lobby for the rights of asylum seekers and refugees until I worked there. I have met the most caring people ever and I would not swap them for anyone! They are now my family and I love every minute of my stay with them. I tell you I have a huge family in the Medical Foundation and the Refugee Council: Dr Jamie (the late Dr Susan's husband) and his children, Sophie, Meg and Ted; Sophie, my mentor, and her parents; and Diana Briscoe. I can't mention everyone but I love them all and I owe them my life! Unfortunately, Dr Susan passed on in 2004 and I still miss her a lot. Her husband, Jamie, her three children and Mary are still helping me to come to terms with her death. I still go to the Medical Foundation to see Mary because I feel vulnerable, and I am in a group with Sheila and Maria called 'Write to Life', which is helping me and my friends with our writing. I have been with other writers on the Arvon Course in Devon, and went to Reading University in March 2007 to meet some women and read my work to them. I am very lucky to be alive and able to attend all these brilliant events.

After a month, the Red Cross gave me an interview. Retelling was still as painful as the day they took my children away from me and took me and my friends forcefully to the bush. The lady I spoke to promised me they would look for my kids, but since the north of Uganda is not a safe place even for the Red Cross, it is taking a long time. But they usually write to tell me about their progress, which gives me some hope that one day, even if they don't find my children, they might find out what happened to them, so that I can mourn them or cuddle them.

I was told to report to the Home Office every week and, as I was still living with Juliet and Andrew in Brockley Road, I started reporting at a place near London Bridge. I had to leave the house around 5 a.m. to be there early, because of the long queue; standing for a long time is still a problem for me. Eventually, I was given a house near St George's Hospital to share with another lady. It was the coldest house ever, and it faced a cemetery. Since I was still very ill, I thought I was going to die. The other lady was ill too, but she had friends to go to. As for me, I did not want to burden Juliet and Andrew. So at Christmas 2001, I stayed in the house for three days without electricity, gas or food. When the landlord came, I told him and his wife about it, and an electrician came, but the toilet and the bath were not working. After some time, they transferred us to The Cut in Waterloo, which was still shared accommodation, but it was warm and not facing a cemetery, and each of us had our own bedroom.

Since I was now living in The Cut, Mary booked an appointment with Dr Barbara, whom I saw until I went to live in Balham. But I did not tell Dr Barbara that I had a bone sticking out of my finger, since I did not want to burden anybody with it. I just cut it off with a kitchen knife. I was immune to pain and felt nothing. I still have the scar.

I lived in The Cut for nine months and then I was sent to a hostel in Peckham High Street, where the staff were very kind and helpful. I was still very ill and withdrawn, but they often came to my room to check on me and I think the other residents too. I went out on buses, looking for my children, thinking I might see them in the crowd. This went on for a long time. Even now, at weekends, I travel on buses, looking for them. Maybe one day I will see them.

When my letter for Indefinite Leave to Remain arrived, I wanted to tear it up, because I was afraid it meant I would not find my children. But the man who had signed for it did not give it to me until he had convinced me that it was okay and that if my children were found they could come and join me here in the UK.

Since I had no home or country, I wanted to become a British citizen, as the British people had given me love and shelter. So I studied for the citizenship test and passed it very well. I applied for citizenship and my ceremony took place in February 2007, attended by my most wonderful family from the Refugee Council, Jamie's children, Juliet, Sophie and Claire, whom I study drama with at Morley College. I am now going to apply for a British passport if I can get the money. So my painful journey also has the happiest ending, because I have a country, Britain, and a home!

# Of Mango Trees and Monkeys

*Charmaine Joshua*

It was never intended to be permanent. Just a phase, a time of my life that I would file together with all my other experiences and escapades. The London years, I suppose I would have called them. But sometimes life is like the kaleidoscope I used to play with as a child – one twist and the pattern changes for ever.

I cannot tell the story of where I am today and how it is that I am here without telling the story of what I left behind. Hidden though they are, the roots sustain a tree. When I was a very young child, I used to sit on the concrete steps leading up to our front door, which was a thin sheet of metal, and squint at the setting sun. It made a clanging sound when slammed, that door, and it felt hard and unyielding against my back. I used to stare at the sun and then close my eyes. At first, all I could see was a hot pulsing colour, which reminded me of blood. But then I would see a circle, which I knew was the sun, first purple, then blue. It reminded me of my mother's powder compact, I cannot say why. The shape, I suppose. I never tired of playing this game, staring at the sun with my eyes open, then shut. Perhaps it was in this way that the sun was burnt into my body so that, long after my mind has accepted its loss, my skin and bones still remember the boiling, bubbling, blistering heat of the South African sun.

I was born in a little town called Pietermaritzburg and lived there until I was twenty-three. The town is famed for its beautiful Victorian architecture, but the only architecture I was familiar with was the semi-detached two-bedroomed council home in which I lived with my parents and two sisters. There were a thousand such houses in our district, all squat and rectangular, the only variation the colour of the walls and the little touches of individuality which people stamped on to their homes, such as the red and saffron *katha* and *jhanda* flags Hindu families would erect in their gardens. Otherwise the houses were identical. The doors were made of metal, the walls of cement blocks and the roofs of asbestos. There were no ceilings, so that in summer our house was a furnace, in winter bitterly cold. Neither was there any hot-water supply; my mother boiled our bathwater in a huge drum over an open fire in the backyard.

My memories are of happy days spent playing with neighbourhood friends in our back garden, not so much a garden as a jungle of fruit trees: paw-paws, avocados, mangoes and lemons. In the midst of this wilderness grew a curry leaf tree, which my father cherished and would carefully cover with a drum on winter nights to shield it from the frost. Here we would build mud-pies, decorate them with cosmos or marigolds, and leave them to bake in the sun. Or climb the mulberry tree at the foot of the garden and hide in its branches. Or play hopscotch, hide-and-seek, cowboys and crooks. The constant backdrop to all my childhood memories is the golden sun: a gift which I took for granted.

I grew up in a country obsessed with race and racial classification. There were four main race groups – I knew this even as a very young child. These were, in hierarchical order: whites, coloureds (people of mixed race), Indians and blacks. Each year, the numbers of people who had been reclassified into another race under the Race Classification Act were published in a government gazette, the determining criteria being skin colour and hair texture. The racial classification of a citizen was recorded on the front page of his or her identity document, together with other essential information. Mine read: 'Indian.'

I was a third-generation South African Indian; my grandparents had come from India as children with their parents, who had been brought over as indentured labourers to work on the sugar-cane plantations of Natal. In accordance with the Group Areas Act, I grew up in an exclusively Indian community and attended schools which could only admit Indian children. Living under these conditions, my contact with other races was limited, but I did not realize that this was abnormal. I recall watching my mother bargaining with black fruit-sellers, who came to the Indian districts to trade their produce or to offer their services as domestic cleaners. These *makotis*, as black women were called, wore brightly coloured cloths on their heads, wrapped around like a flat turban, their boxes of fruit perfectly balanced on top as they walked from door to door. The skin on their faces, when not hidden under a layer of reddish clay, was old and gnarled, their ears so pierced that the lower parts hung to their jawbones. Sometimes they asked for food and water, which we gave to them in enamel cups and plates that were clean but which we did not use.

At the other end of the scale, my childhood encounters with white people reinforced the prevailing view of their superiority. When I was about ten years old, my parents bought a washing machine. It needed to be plumbed into the water mains, and a white engineer was sent by the furniture store to do this. All the neighbourhood children crowded into our kitchen to marvel at him as he went about his task, giggling and nudging each other surreptitiously. After he had finished, my father offered him a glass of Fanta, while his assistant, a black, only got water from an enamel cup.

It was at secondary school that I began to question

what I had previously always taken for granted. History lessons were disrupted by incessant interrogations of our teacher as to 'what was the real story' behind the government-endorsed textbooks. Every so often, in response to some new atrocity of apartheid, we would storm out of our classrooms and sit in the school grounds in protest or march around the school chanting angrily. Nothing was achieved; we were ordered back into our classrooms by the police or kept at home by our fearful parents.

My best friend during these turbulent adolescent years was Shakira Shaik. She had dimpled cheeks and laughing eyes, and seemed to be the only person in the entire world who understood how I felt about fundamental issues and felt the same. We shared a passion for English literature; together we would read poetry and discuss the great themes of Shakespeare. While I loved her deeply, I did not seriously consider us to be lesbians. The other students did though, and because she was Muslim, a group of Muslim girls visited her parents to tell them what they thought was going on. Shakira was kept home for a day or two and, when she returned, she ignored me completely. At breaktimes, she huddled together with the other Muslim girls, their *ijaars* and *burkas* closing them off from me.

At the tender age of twenty-three, having graduated from the local university, which I had been able to attend with a bursary, I accepted an offer of employment from a large law firm in Johannesburg, and left my little town for the big city. My father had tears in his eyes when he hugged me goodbye in my little flat in Hillbrow, one of Johannesburg's seedier suburbs, before driving the 500 kilometres back to my home town. That night, my first away from the family home, was long and dark and filled with the strange street sounds of a violent city. I covered my head with my blanket and waited for the dawn. It was a rehearsal for a greater separation to come, for in that same year I won a scholarship to study abroad at a university of my choice.

So miraculous did the idea of my going overseas seem that my mother could not believe it until she saw an article with my picture in the local newspaper. Later, my father made a copy of the article, which he framed in our lounge and proudly showed to visitors.

I had chosen to enrol in a master's programme at Cambridge – a university my family had never heard of before – partly because there was a precedent of South African law graduates doing so but mainly because, all through my childhood, England had been the land of my dreams. When I was very young, my sisters would read me stories with brightly coloured pictures of castles, forests, princesses and fairies. They always told me that these pictures were of England. Later, England became the land of the Famous Five, and later still, of Thomas Hardy, Jane Austen and Shakespeare. And what greater fairy tale could there be than royalty? As a child, I had stood in a jam-packed prefab classroom to watch the wedding of Charles and Diana on a tiny black and white television which our teacher had brought in for the occasion. Imagine the impact that the image of a horse-drawn glass carriage and the towering dome of St Paul's Cathedral had on children growing up in a slum, the vast majority of whom would be working in a shoe factory by the age of eighteen. It was magic.

I hated Cambridge. I had arrived in mid September, a week before the start of the academic year, and grew steadily more depressed as the days shortened and became colder and wetter. I once counted fifteen days of incessant gloom without any sunshine. To feel some connection with home, I would call each night from the payphone in the kitchen of the house I shared with four other graduate students, and I would listen to my mother, or my father or my boyfriend saying, 'Hello, hello,' just for a few seconds before the line was disconnected.

I had been granted a scholarship of 60,000 rand, which seemed a large amount in rand but not when converted into sterling. Like most of the other foreign students, the basis on which I calculated the cost of living in the UK was the exchange rate, then roughly five rand to the pound. So a sandwich which cost two pounds would set me back ten rand. Prices were one thing, but how to compare pounds with kilograms? And how does one go about buying something as simple as breakfast cereal when there are two aisles full of different brands to choose from? For the first few weeks, I lived chiefly off sandwiches made from white bread and baked beans from Sainsbury's. Once I tried to buy plums in Market Square, but the only word I could pick out from what the stall-holder was shouting at me was 'love', so I panicked and left, dropping the bag of fruit. Gradually, shopping became easier and I noticed that food, especially junk food, was cheaper in the UK than back home. Fruit and vegetables cost about the same, but in the UK there was a much greater variety. Red meat and fish were a lot more expensive, but as I didn't cook much I didn't buy those anyway. And I stopped buying sausages when one of the German students in my college pointed out that the label said '60 per cent real meat'; in the light of the mad cow scare, I was nervous about what the other 40 per cent might be.

Only one of the other students in the house I lived in was English. He kept to himself mostly; the three foreigners and I would often share meals and chat together. I got on best with Younus, a Bengali chemist. His English was poor but we had a common Indian heritage, which manifested itself in food. I was completely undomesticated and content to live off sandwiches and scrambled eggs. But every evening when Younus returned home, he would wash, don his *dhoti* and flip-flops and hasten to the kitchen, singing to himself. He would set the rice to boil, then chat with me while he chopped up onions, ginger, garlic and vegetables. As the rice bubbled and his hands worked, he would tell me tales of Dhaka, of his family and his girlfriend back home. A few times, he would stop working and fall silent, and his eyes would roll up as he became caught up in the memory of the story he was recounting. I thought then that he was reliving the sounds and smells and tastes of all he had left behind. That perhaps, for a moment, he was feeling himself there again. That the spasm of separation was so intense that he could only give himself up to it and let it wash over him.

Before I had left South Africa, everyone had told me what a golden opportunity it was to be able to study at Cambridge and how I should make the most of it. Though I tried to convince myself that I was having a fantastic time, I could not overcome the cold in my bones and the ache in my heart. Immediately after finishing my exams, I returned home to South Africa.

It was a strange homecoming. From the moment the plane touched down at Johannesburg, all the way through passport control and the drive to my boyfriend's flat downtown, I had a feeling of anticlimax.

Even watching the sun set did not ease my sense of disquiet. All those many months I had spent at Cambridge longing to be at home, but now that I was here finally, it did not feel like home at all. Two days later, I boarded a bus to Pietermaritzburg, longing to be in my childhood home. I slept through much of the 5-hour journey, but awoke just as the bus was heading down the steep hills of Howick and Hilton, about fifteen kilometres or so from the town. I have always loved this part of the world; on either side of the highway, soft green hills merge into each other, resembling bread rolls baking in the sunshine. But for me, even the landscape had changed and was not quite as beautiful as I remembered it.

As the bus rolled into the depot, I looked eagerly out of the window, trying unsuccessfully to spot my parents. And then I saw my mum. I remember noticing that the dress she wore looked old and shabby, while, simultaneously, my mind registered that the man standing next to her must be my dad. My sisters had written to tell me that he was not well, but I had not expected this. In the space of nine months, he had aged ten years. He looked gaunt and weary, his hair sparse, his face unshaven. As I got off the bus, he did not even try to pick up my suitcase; it was as if he recognized that it would be too much for him.

Later that day, settled in the old bedroom which I had once shared with my sisters, I felt a deep sadness as I looked around the room at the uneven unplastered walls, at the cheap polyester bedding and the stains on the lino. I had never really noticed before how small and poor and shabby my home was. It had always been filled with the voices and laughter of my sisters and niece; now it was so quiet. The sadness was mixed with guilt that I had lived in relative comfort in Cambridge, that in Johannesburg I mixed with colleagues who knew nothing of such poverty, that I inhabited worlds which my parents could never be part of. I felt that I was betraying my parents by being part of that world.

My father was a gentle man who would whistle as he went about his chores, but when he was angered he would grind his teeth and clench his fists. He had retired from work two years previously, and it was as if he had retired from life itself. Like me, my sisters had flown the nest, so the house was empty, the days long and empty too. My mother explained that my father's heart condition had deteriorated in the past few months; even the short trip from his bed to the toilet rendered him so short of breath that he had taken to using a chamber pot. It was horrible to see this decline: my love was reduced to pity, shame and guilt, even anger. I read Dylan Thomas's 'Do Not Go Gentle into That Good Night' to him, to try to provoke a reaction, but all I got was a smile. I don't think he was listening to the words, only to my voice. Once or twice during my visit, we talked about Cambridge and I showed him my photographs and he said it looked beautiful, but I think he feigned interest, and I found it difficult to bridge the divide. I wish now that I had made more of an effort. When, a week later, I boarded the bus back to Johannesburg, it was with an overpowering sadness but also relief, and guilt because of it.

My father died three months later, on my twenty-fifth birthday. Two years later, I accepted a position at a London law firm.

Why did I choose to return to the UK? Because at the law firm where I worked in Johannesburg, I was still sometimes mistaken for a tea lady. Because my father, who used to call white men 'boss', had died in a third-rate hospital reserved for Indians. Because you can abolish a law, but you cannot change how people think or erase the prejudice behind it. Because the belonging I felt in the country of my birth had turned to displacement, and in my heart I was restless and angry and searching for some comfort for my sorrow.

My memories of that first week in London are mainly of the chaos and clamour of the underground: so many people, all moving so quickly, pushing me along, no time to read signs, the screeching trains drowning out any attempt to seek directions. In the midst of the masses, I felt like a bystander, alone and unnoticed in a large impersonal city which seemed to rush along in a constant blur. Disembarking from a train during the morning rush hour, map in hand, attempting to plot my route amid the noise and haste, I had an absurd urge to shout out: 'Stop! I'm here, I'm here.'

Arriving in February, I had braced myself for the cold and wet, but knowing something in your mind is never the same as enduring it in the flesh. Rainy mornings were so uncommon when I was a child that my mother used to keep me home from school. Now I would have to go to work in the rain. Every day I would mutter under my breath as I trudged along to the Tube station with hundreds of fellow commuters in the grey gloom and fine drizzle. Even the rain here is different, I often observed, recalling the drama and violence of thunderstorms back home, and cursing this meek drip-drip-drip which went on and on and on. At the station, I would wait on an above-ground platform where the wind blew so cold it brought tears to my eyes and snot to my nose, only to hear 'we are currently experiencing delays on the Jubilee Line' over the tannoy.

By far the greatest shock was the cost of accommodation. The firm had put me up in a flat for the first two weeks, but after that I was on my own. Not knowing anyone to share with, I was easy prey for estate agents and ended up paying a quarter of my salary for a dingy one-bedroomed flat in a house

I was told was in West Hampstead but was actually in Kilburn. There was no central heating, and at night the glass of water on my bedside table would ice over. But I soon became friendly with one of the tenants in the flat above, N, an aspiring actress of mixed Irish and West Indian ancestry, with chiselled cheekbones and a mass of dark curls, who would gently mimic what she called my 'colonial tones'. Like me, N was new to London. She would often pop in for a cup of tea and we would sit together and mope over how expensive everything was. One day, she got into an argument with the people at the Royal Academy: insisting that art should be free, she had refused to pay the entrance fee and had been frogmarched out of the building. Needless to say, I loved her.

The law firm I worked at was huge, a thousand lawyers and a few thousand support staff, all housed in an intimidating glass and granite building. On my first day, I was given a security pass which I was told to carry with me at all times; I soon found that I could not even get to the toilet without it. While the firm was on the whole made up of white male lawyers, the department I was in was made up largely of Asian, Italian and Antipodean lawyers. The head of the department was a Gujearati whose family had fled Uganda during the 1970s. For once, I was as different as everyone else. In this way, it was wonderful.

In other ways, it was bewildering. In South Africa,

as a qualified lawyer, I was served tea in my office by our tea lady, Albertina, whose face radiated kindness and who always had time for a laugh. Here, I had to get it myself from a machine or from the coffee shop in the basement. In my old firm, lawyers had to address partners as 'Mr so-and-so'; here, I found that not only did partners have to share offices like everyone else, they were also addressed by their first names. I could not do this easily, and addressed the partner I worked for as 'Mr M' until he told me, quite firmly, to call him by his first name. But worse was to come. After my first week, he invited me to lunch at the Pizza Express across the road. In South Africa, if a lawyer was invited to lunch by a partner, it was accepted that the partner would pay, so I did not even think to take my wallet. When the bill arrived, I smiled and thanked him for lunch. He said nothing. It was only later that I learnt from my roommate that, in London, this was unacceptably rude. I still cringe at the memory.

My roommate, S, was a Kenyan Indian with large bulbous eyes, a regal demeanour and a mercurial temperament: one minute she would be stroking her neck dreamily, the next she would be raging, her eyes dark and flashing, her nostrils quivering. The thing in which S took the greatest delight was my inexperience of life in London. Like a rotting carcass to a hyena, this was meat off which she fed for many days. Every mistake, however slight, was immediately detected, exaggerated and ridiculed. How embarrassing it was to be the constant butt of her little jokes. But then, just when it became unbearable, she would smile and croon, 'Oh, sweetie, you're not cross, are you, honey?'

February became March, March, April; colleagues became friends and, bit by bit, things started falling into place. I realized that it was quicker to get off the Circle Line at Mansion House and walk to Aldersgate than to stay on until Farringdon. I learnt that pants meant underwear, not trousers, that the word for pantyhose was tights. I discovered peppermint foot lotion from Body Shop and cinnamon-flavoured chocolate from Thorntons. At night, scurrying down Cheapside, I would gaze at the dome of St Paul's, dazed and dazzled that I was here among streets and sights that were centuries-old. Weekends, I would wander the little warren of alleys in Soho, mesmerized by the roast ducks hanging in the restaurant windows in Chinatown. Sometimes I would go to a pub called the North Pole; it was the only one I knew how to get to without getting lost. Here, on my own, I would sip a shandy, enjoying the loud music and the atmosphere and wishing for someone to share this grand adventure with.

And then suddenly, one May morning, without word or warning but with a whoosh and a bang, the sun is bright and the air is fresh and the light as pure as in a great glass bubble, and there are tiny pale flowers on the trees (why did I never notice them before?), and I am singing as I walk to work, and everyone is smiling, and I am eating Pret sandwiches in St Paul's churchyard on the green, green grass with my best, best friend Shakira Shaik, and I have never felt so alive and so happy and surely, surely there can be no finer place than this in all the world?

I am not sure that I would have stayed on in London but for those two miracles: the explosion of my first English summer and the reunion with my childhood friend Shakira, whom I bumped into, literally, in Soho. My friend had renamed herself Sabina, after the character in Milan Kundera's *The Unbearable Lightness of Being*, and had left South Africa to take up a teaching position at a school for children with severe learning difficulties. She told me that she had finally accepted that she was a lesbian, that this was who she chose to be and that she could not continue trying to be otherwise just to please her Muslim family. It was only in London, living under the anonymity which London gifts to its inhabitants, that Sabina was fully free to choose and acknowledge her sexual identity.

I have lived in London for the past ten years, seven of which have been spent married to a British-born Chinese. Five years ago, my sister and her family moved to London, bringing my mother with her. It is only my eldest sister who still lives in South Africa, my one tie to a country that is home only in my memories.

Like my mother, I am a wife with two young children, whom I feed and bathe and nurture. Sabina is my closest friend and godmother to my daughter. Though we hardly see each other – she lives in north London, I in the south – I cannot imagine life without her. I work part-time in an office and part of the time at home, where I sing to my children tales of mango trees and monkeys or of the glories of a South African thunderstorm.

Sometimes, in a quiet moment during my busy day, perhaps when I am washing up my baby's bottles at my kitchen sink or walking home from the school run, I find myself bathed in a shaft of sunlight, and I stop and remember who I am and where I come from. I marvel that my grandparents voyaged across the Indian Ocean to a far-off land, yet my father never travelled more than 500 kilometres from his home. I marvel at my piecemeal life, each little episode interlocking into the next like so many bits of a jigsaw, each event in the chain triggered either by choice or by coincidence. And I marvel at all the doors that were closed and had to be prised open, at all the random decisions that could so easily have gone the other way, at all the roads not taken. When, in such moments, I squeeze my eyes shut and remember the circle of the sun against my eyelids and the cold hard metal against my back, it is all I can do to stop myself from crying.

My children will grow up in a country where they cannot be made less than they are. They will never carry the stigma and shame of third-class citizenship. They may face bullying and taunting and even racial discrimination – no child of ethnic minority is spared this in even the most liberal of nations – but it is not the law, it is not the norm, it is not the natural order of things. And is that not worth all the sunshine in the world?

# Notes on the Authors

## Jade Amoli-Jackson

My twin sister, Jane, and I were born in northern
Uganda on 2 August 1948. I studied journalism at
Makerere University and went on to work as a sports
reporter on Ugandan television, radio and local
papers. My sister and father were killed by Ugandan
government soldiers, and I fled Uganda when my life
was in danger. I arrived in the UK in July 2001. I was
referred to the Medical Foundation because I had
been tortured. I started seeing doctors, a therapist, a
psychiatrist and a physiotherapist, and I have now
joined Write to Life. I am very happy as I have
understanding friends, who have also suffered at the
hands of bad people. I have been a volunteer at
the Refugee Council since July 2005.

## Mimi Chan-Choong

I was born in 1947 in Karlovy Vary in the Czech Republic and now live in Fulmer, Buckinghamshire. I am a retired teacher, although I spent much of my life as a part-time shopkeeper, running a deli, a souvenir shop and a wool shop. My husband, Michael Chan-Choong, is from Guyana in South America and we have two grown-up children. I enjoy learning languages and love to travel, which offers me the opportunity to practise my new skills. Since communism fell in Czechoslovakia, my mother and I travel back to see our family regularly – so I don't forget my Czech!

## Xenia Crockett

I was born in Germany, came to England aged fifteen, and lived in London for twelve years before moving to Berkshire with Ron, my husband of nearly fifty years now.

At seventy-three, I have the freedom to actually put pen to paper. I write for the joy of it – currently a story about witches for children. My dream is to record my family's varied life stories for my four children and five grandchildren, perhaps illustrated with photos and drawings. Retirement means enjoying what I like most: gardening, travelling, writing, reading and needlework.

## Toni Jackson

I was born in Glasgow in 1950 and left school at sixteen to go to college to train as a nursery nurse. Since childhood, I have enjoyed writing poetry and short stories. I lead a contented life in Glasgow, with my husband and son, the youngest of our five children.

## Kirti Joshi

I was born in Kampala and was forced to leave when Amin told us to go. I am thirty-five years old and divorced. I have a son who is fifteen years old. I was brought up in Leicester, where I still live to this day. I am very proud to be Hindu and I love my heritage, but I also love western culture. I enjoy socializing, theatre and books.

## Nina Joshi

At age eleven, in Nairobi, after scribbling for hours in a huge hall with lots of other children, I won my first writing competition. I wondered if such a job as writing all day existed. Duty called, I studied IT and eventually joined Reuters as a graduate trainee, where, along with management skills, I gained a fascination for unbiased news, a bountiful social circle and, later, even a husband. Now, under the compelling mentorship of Fay Weldon, I am writing a novel for a creative writing MA at Brunel University. I collect *Paris Reviews* and dispense copies of Tagore's *Gitanjali*, for its life-enriching properties.

## Charmaine Joshua

I was born in 1969 in Pietermaritzburg, South Africa, to second-generation South African Indians and lived through some of the dark days of the apartheid era and its demise, which haunt and inspire me still. I have degrees in law and English literature, which is my first and foremost passion. I worked as a lawyer in Johannesburg before moving to London, where I now live with my husband and two children.

## Marek Kazmierski

Born in Warszawa, Poland, I came to the UK in 1985, graduated in English literature and comparative religion and, having decided to become a writer, I spent the last decade accumulating enough experience to have something to write about. This has included stints as a labourer, teacher, security guard, stripper, translator, salesman, restaurateur and librarian. Today, I keep busy writing, filming, painting, coordinating cultural/diversity affairs for the Home Office and running three voluntary arts organizations, including a writers' group in north London.

## Vesna Maric

I was born in Bosnia-Herzegovina in 1976 and came to the UK at the age of sixteen, and lived in the Lake District, Devon and Yorkshire before moving in 1997 to London, a city I love. I write travel guides and still live in London, with my partner, Rafael.

## Cosh Omar

I was born on the Bishops Avenue, Finchley, in north London, but spent the first ten years of my life living in White Hart Lane, Tottenham. Then it was off to much more middle-class (and Cypriot) Palmers Green. After leaving school, I travelled around America and Europe, doing various jobs before deciding to audition for drama school. I have since been existing in the precarious world of acting and playwriting. I am now living in what seems like the heart of suburbia, leafy Southgate, right at the end of the Piccadilly line. I have the honour of being joined there by my wife, Sonal, my son, Izzet, and daughter, Leyla.

## Zlatko Pranjic

I arrived in London from Zagreb in September 1993. During the civil war, I worked for various newspapers as a journalist. After my arrest by a nationalist state faction, I was evacuated from Croatia as part of an official programme organized by the UN. In London, I am involved in theatre and have recently helped to establish a new company called Theatre With Accent.

## Menaka Raman

I was born in 1980 in Thuvakudi, a small town in the south Indian state of Tamil Nadu. My family's nomadic ways took me to Madras, Hong Kong, Abu Dhabi and London. At the age of eleven, I returned to Madras and ten years later, I found myself with a bachelor's degree in computer science. Destiny had other plans for me and I became an advertising copywriter. Marriage took me to Bombay and, two years ago, brought me to London. Last year, I quit advertising and since then I have been volunteering with Action Against Hunger and writing short stories.

## Nimer Rashed

I was born in London and, after various stints in New York, rural Japan and the south of France, I've ended up living just off the Kilburn High Road, which is the most exciting place of all. Last year, I won the Sir Peter Ustinov Scriptwriting Award at New York's International Emmy Awards and second place in Soho Theatre's Westminster Prize. I spend my days reading scripts and novels for various film companies and my nights writing scripts and novels for fun. One day, I hope to sleep.

## Anita Sethi

I was born in Manchester in 1981 and read English at Cambridge University. I am now a journalist, contributing to the *Guardian* and various other publications, including the *New Statesman*, *The Times Literary Supplement*, the *Independent*, the *Sunday Times* and the *Daily Telegraph*. I received an Arts Council writing award to complete a novel I am working on and have had poetry published in several magazines.

## Ali Sheikholeslami

The axis of evil, that's where I was born. Not that I claim that nationality per se is a matter of either importance or interest to me. I was born after a revolution and before a war. I was born when oil – as always – was the biggest problem. I grew up with the soothing sound of air-attack sirens. I had to put up with drastic policies and politics after the war, but that didn't stop me from getting excited about the reforms in the late 1990s. I have witnessed madness in the world, the power obsession that makes one side of the world the axis of evil and the other side the great Satan. And now, here I am . . . with a passport that can wipe the slightest trace of a smile off any immigration officer's face.

## Cliff Walker

I was born in Antigua some sixty-six years ago, and am married with three grown-up children and six grandchildren, all living in Cambridgeshire. I have lived in the UK for over fifty years, half of which were spent in the Royal Air Force, which allowed me to travel to many countries. Before I retired, I spent fifteen years as a civil servant, working for the Ministry of Defence. Now I am very involved in community affairs and was awarded the MBE some years ago. I am also a Deputy Lieutenant of Cambridgeshire. But the joy of my life is being with my grandchildren.